THIS IS YOUR BRAIN
ON SPORTS

Beating blocks, slumps and performance anxiety for good!

By Dr. David Grand & Dr. Alan Goldberg

First published by Dog Ear Publishing
4010 W. 86th Street, Ste H
Indianapolis, IN 46268
www.dogearpublishing.net

ISBN: 978-160844-864-7

This book is printed on acid-free paper.

Printed in the United States of America

ACKNOWLEDGMENTS

A book such as this does not come into being without the efforts of many people. First and foremost we would like to thank Rob Polishook, the "Third Musketeer" on our team. Rob has been instrumental and supportive in the development of Brainspotting Sports Performance Work, the Sports Trauma Model and the application of our theories to on the court and in the field work. Rob has also been the key person in helping us make connections with Mackey Sasser and Howard Smith. Rob is also a marketing genius and an unstoppable force. This leads us to Mackey Sasser who we are proud to call a friend and supporter. Mackey opened himself to our work and helped demonstrate that even the most "locked up" athlete can be unlocked". Mackey serves as an inspiration and advocate, and his efforts have and will bring relief and freedom to countless suffering, frozen gifted athletes.

Big thanks to Howard Smith of MLB for being open to big ideas and being willing to give us his support and backing. Howard was never too busy to step in for us to open a door that otherwise might have remained closed. Thanks to Lisa Schwarz as a Brainspotting pioneer in the area of Sports Dissociation. Her work in this area is seminal and has become a foundation of the Sports Trauma Model. Much appreciation to Bob Scaer who has brought his wonderful innovations to the field of trauma and its treatment. We are proud to have Bob as a supporter and friend. Thanks to Calder Kaufmann who represents the future of our work. Calder is a gifted pitcher/psychologist who will ably carry our work into the future. Gratitude to Uri Bergmann for being a teacher and guide in his neurobiological wisdom. Thanks to the folks at Dog Ear Press who are there to make books like ours a reality. Appreciation to Dave Larabel of Black Agency for believing in us and for his efforts on our book's behalf. We value the team which has been behind us on the journey for the years: Esly Carvalho, Chris Ranck, Martha Jacobi, Pie Frey, Diane Israel, Roberto Weisz, Steve Walker, Earl Poteet, Laura Hillesheim, Ceri Evans, Shane Crain, Deb Antinori, Linda Brennan, Lucy Brown, Neilly Buckalew, Anne Buford, Sjoerd de Jongh, Susan Dowell, Kevin Dowling, Philip Dutton, Chloe Katz, Chaya Kaufmann, Oliver Schubbe, Mario Salvador, Fran Yoeli, Evan Seinfeld, Tom Taylor and Terrie Williams.

Last but surely not least, we would like to thank our many athlete-clients who have put their trust in us, shared their pain and taught us so much about resiliency and the journey from blocks to breakthroughs. We especially would like to thank those individuals who have so willingly allowed us to share their stories with you.

CONTENT

INTRODUCTION

We met for dinner on Friday night in a bistro on the upper west side of Manhattan. It was Mackey Sasser's birthday. The next day had been arranged to tackle the impossible: freeing him from the throwing "yips" that had put an end to his Major League career 11 years earlier. We avoided talking about the impending challenge and instead shared laughs and war stories from the baseball diamond and sports psychology office. Mackey exuded affability and southern charm, but he couldn't mask his keen intellect and deep soulfulness from a couple of shrinks like us.

At 6'1", 210 lbs, Mackey Sasser was the catcher of the future for the 1988 New York Mets. An aggressive hitter, Sasser was surprisingly agile for a catcher. The Mets had acquired him to replace the aging Gary Carter. In his rookie season, Sasser batted .285 with an on-base percentage of .313. His numbers steadily improved over the next two years. In 1990, Sasser hit .307 and was a lock as a starter and a potential all-star.

Despite his strength both behind the plate and at bat, all was not right with Sasser. In his rookie season, Mackey occasionally struggled with the simple task of throwing the ball back to the pitcher. Sasser began to double, triple, and even quadruple pump the ball before releasing it. When he finally let it go, his toss back was a soft flip rather than a hard throw. Opposing runners took advantage of this pre-throw idiosyncrasy and timed their delayed steals to Sasser's pumping motion.

Mackey's problem was especially confusing, as he had no trouble throwing back to the pitcher *in the bullpen* or nailing a runner

From l-r, David Grand, Mackey Sasser, Rob Polishook and
Alan Goldberg at Shea Stadium, summer 2008)

Mackey during his Mets days

attempting to steal second base. In 1990, his best year in the majors, Sasser's throwing difficulties worsened. The New York fans and media responded with cruelty; "Sasser syndrome" had hit the Big Apple. "Sasser's throwing his career away," headlined the sports pages. He was the butt of relentless jokes, and during games, the hometown fans would loudly count in unison, "ONE! TWO! THREE!" each time Mackey pumped the ball. His fear and humiliation became so intense that Sasser panicked the night before every game.

Mackey desperately tried to solve his problem on his own, yet all his efforts proved futile. The countless experts he consulted fared no better in reversing his downward spiral. None of it made any sense to him. How was it possible that in a sport in which he had excelled his entire life, being the MVP at every level he played at, he couldn't execute the simplest of athletic tasks?

The final blow came in 1990 when Sasser was bowled over by the Braves' Jim Presley while blocking home plate. Sasser landed on the disabled list for six weeks and was never the same. His hitting dropped off, and he couldn't release the ball at all. He saw less and less action behind the plate and was ultimately released in November 1992. Mackey was quickly signed by the Mariners, but soon, his throwing problem was back in full force, so he opted out of the defensive lineup. In 1995, after brief stints with the Padres and Pirates, Sasser retired. He returned home to Alabama as head coach of his alma mater, Wallace Community College.

When we first met Mackey in the summer of 2006, he was still saddled with this inexplicable throwing disorder. When throwing batting practice to his players, he couldn't release or control the ball. The 19-year-old problem was blocking him from coaching in the majors, a dream Sasser had carried since he had retired. Mackey shared, "I could be a damn good bullpen coach in the bigs, but I'd have to throw batting practice. I'm afraid I couldn't cut it and face that humiliation again."

Our goal in meeting with Mackey was simple. We aimed to help him resolve his much-publicized throwing yips and demonstrate Brainspotting Sport's Work groundbreaking power in resolving Repetitive Sports Performance Problems (RSPPs). We couldn't help Mackey get his big-league career back, but we aspired to heal his yips, liberating him to throw batting practice.

I (Alan Goldberg) have been working exclusively in the field of applied sports psychology for more than 26 years, specializing in helping athletes like Sasser overcome performance fears and blocks. In 1997, I wrote *Sports Slump Busting*, which featured my successful model for healing athletes struggling with RSPPs. Despite my success over the years, I just couldn't help certain athletes. I sensed I was missing something that could push my work to another level. My search for answers led me to the work of David Grand, a New York trauma therapist and an internationally known expert on creativity and performance enhancement. The author of *Emotional Healing at Warp Speed—The Power of EMDR,* David had applied trauma-healing techniques to performance blocks and pioneered a method that transcended every approach currently utilized in sports psychology. His theories were groundbreaking: All repetitive sports-performance problems, like the yips and severe slumps, have trauma bases that operate outside the athlete's conscious awareness and control, and unless the underlying physical and emotional traumas are determined and directly addressed, the block might reduce but not fully release.

David had been refining his methods for many years with actors, singers, and dancers as well as athletes. After watching his work and training with him, I believed that his approach was the piece that I was missing. My work with Amanda, a level-9 gymnast paralyzed by fear (see Chapter 6), was proof that David's approach would revolutionize sports psychology. Amanda had suffered a serious accident on the uneven bars the year before I began working with her and had never recovered emotionally. In the past, I would have had limited success working with her; supervised by David, however, I helped Amanda *completely* conquer her fear and return to top form.

Over the past four years, we have combined Dr. Grand's approach and my Slump Busting expertise, with the result being the book you are reading right now. Because the bulk of our theory and techniques stem directly from David, we have adopted his Brainspotting Sports Work name.

When David and I began creating a practical book about this groundbreaking method, we wanted to work with an athlete who could demonstrate the power of this revolutionary approach. We learned that Mackey Sasser's publicized throwing problem was still active despite the efforts of more than 50 professionals during his playing days. We felt that he would be a perfect candidate. Mackey was also eager to meet with us, hoping to gain clarity and perspective on his personal, recurring nightmare.

Our initial meeting with Mackey was orchestrated by Rob Polishook, sports performance coach and personal friend. Rob's pursuit of a career in sports psychology had initially led him to contact David and then me. Through a connection with a friend in Major League Baseball, Rob arranged our meeting with Mackey. First, the four of us got together on Friday night for dinner, followed by the session conducted by David the next day. David started by taking an extensive personal and sports-trauma history and then did five hours of amazing Brainspotting Sports Work healing with Mackey. This initial session was followed up by two brief phone sessions and then a trip to Dothan, Alabama, to work with Mackey and a number of his college players.

When we visited Mackey in Alabama eight months after our first meeting, Mackey was able to comfortably throw batting practice without hesitation. His 19-year performance problem was finally over! Mackey shared with us, "I can just go out and throw with no problem, even in front of a big crowd. It's like a five hundred-pound weight was lifted from my shoulders."

People in and out of the sports field are unaware that Mackey's career-ending condition is part of a *silent epidemic* crippling athletes at every level of every sport, yet coaches, parents, and athletes are afraid to talk about it as if it might be contagious. As in Mackey's case, the yips appear to emerge out of the blue: a control pitcher loses his accuracy, a golfer's wrists jerk on the green, a gymnast balks on a skill she's been nailing for years, a basketball player misses free throws with seconds on the clock, a tennis player double faults at break point, or a diver mysteriously loses his ability to throw a reverse one and a half.

The onset of these RSPPs never makes sense to the athlete, coaches, parents, or fans. The athlete hasn't a clue what's really wrong and is at a loss about how to "fix" it. His or her best efforts lead to more frustration and a deepening of the struggles. The athlete's coaches try everything they know in a futile attempt to get the athlete back on track. When they fail, coaches feel helpless and overwhelmed and often end up deeming the athlete a "head case." Some coaches then subject the athlete to further emotional turmoil with humiliations in front of teammates. RSPPs can be tenacious, defying the best efforts of most professionals. The athlete, unable to perform like he or she did before, often prematurely quits his or her sport in defeat.

Similar woes have plagued high-profile athletes like pitchers Steve Blass, Rick Ankiel, and Mark Wohlers; infielder Chuck Knoblauch; and golfers David Duval and Ben Hogan. For each famous name, countless unknown athletes are suffering the same fate: child, high school, and collegiate athletes, as well as world-class and pro competitors.

What's happening, and what can be done to help these struggling athletes return to top form? Coaches, teammates, fans, and the media freely offer their opinions on what is "really" wrong. By doing so, they have added to the tremendous misunderstanding that already exists by saying things like, "He's mentally weak," "She's just not motivated," "He's cursed," "She doesn't want it bad enough," "He's a choker," and "She's a quitter."

Every sport has a name for these mysterious RSPPs. In baseball, for pitchers, they're called Steve Blass Disease, after the 1971 World Series MVP who suddenly and irretrievably lost his trademark control. For catchers, they're referred to as Sasser Syndrome. In golf and now in other sports, they're labeled the yips. In archery and shooting sports, they're called target panic. In competitive darts, dartitis; in gymnastics, cheerleading, and diving, they're called balking.

Traditional sports psychologists have typically confined their work with RSPPs to the surface of the problem, focusing on the athlete's conscious mental strategies. They apply behavioral techniques to guide the athlete to relax under pressure, change his or her negative self-talk, focus on the task at hand, mentally rehearse peak performance, let go of mistakes, and quiet an overactive mind.

Although all these surface strategies are certainly useful for mental-toughness training and a *necessary* part of an athlete's skill set, they consistently fall short when it comes to releasing RSPPs. These cognitive techniques bring partial, temporary relief to the athlete because they address only the *symptoms of the problem* (pre-performance nervousness, negative thinking, or poor focus, for example); however, they leave the roots untouched, and consequently, the performance difficulties remain or eventually reemerge.

I learned this the hard way in my work with gymnasts and divers. Both sports have an inherently high fear factor because of their degree of difficulty and physical risk. To progress through the ranks and learn new tricks and dives, one must first fail repeatedly in the learning process. Unlike other sports, in which mistakes have minimal consequences, in gymnastics and diving, making mistakes while learning leaves one emotionally and physically shaken, bruised, and, at times, injured.

Lindsey Dutton doing layout dismount

Blocked athletes in gymnastics and diving continually described their experiences to us in phrases like "my brain is stuck" or "the fear is in the back of my mind" or "I can't get my body to go for it." Unlike those we could help effectively with surface strategies, these athletes couldn't seem to utilize conscious, mental toughness techniques . *The fear that gripped them was so all-consuming that conscious self-talk, mental imagery, concentration, and relaxation techniques weren't useful or relevant in positively addressing their nervousness and frozenness.*

These stuck athletes were suffering from a version of post-traumatic stress disorder (PTSD) that we have labeled *sports traumatic stress disorder* (STSD). The source of the athletes' deep fears and blocks could be traced to their trauma and injury history both inside and outside their sports.

Playing sports exposes us to both physical and emotional trauma. In fact, daily life makes us vulnerable to frequent negative experiences, some greater than others. When we play competitive sports, our exposure to these kinds of physical and emotional traumas increases. Sports like gymnastics, diving, football, and ice hockey carry a higher potential for more serious injuries than others.

Physical traumas can be as basic as a mild sprained ankle, a slightly pulled muscle, or the wind being knocked out of us by a collision. Physical traumas, however, can be more serious and include concussions, torn cartilage, broken or dislocated bones, deep lacerations, and any injury requiring surgery. These traumas can occur either on or off the field.

Emotional sports trauma can include humiliation from an abusive coach, teammate, or parent; choking that causes the athlete's team a crucial loss; or frightening, serious or painful physical injuries (a beaning, for example). Sometimes the trauma results from witnessing a serious injury to another athlete.

When we examine the sports and personal histories of athletes struggling with RSPPs, we *always* find an accumulation of these sports traumas. With STSD, these physical and emotional traumas are frozen in the athlete's brain and body. This includes all the images, sounds, emotions, body sensations, and negative thinking that accompany the traumas.

This contrasts to how our brain and body deal with normal experiences. Most daily events are processed through and stored in our deep brain far from consciousness. If you recall them, they elicit little or no physical or emotional reaction. Because trauma memories are frozen in their entirety, they block athletes from connecting with positive past experiences. A softball pitcher intellectually knows her odds of getting hit in the face *again* are slim, yet her heightened fear about it blocks her

Sports trauma

access to this fact, so she can't break through her anxiety, can't relax and focus on the mound, and is unable to throw with speed and accuracy. Her physical and emotional memories of the trauma, held outside of her awareness, are re-triggered every time she pitches. As a consequence, she fails in her attempts to use positive self-talk, visualization, rituals, concentration, and relaxation techniques. For athletes faced with trauma-fueled performance problems, these strategies feel like trying to stop a charging elephant with a butterfly net.

As an athlete sustains additional traumas, these frozen negative experiences *unconsciously* accumulate. ***It's the unconscious remnants of these previous negative performance experiences that generate the sense of danger, physical tension, and self-doubt that interfere with optimal performance.*** These traumatic roots remain untouched by today's cognitive sports-psychology approach because the regular approach addresses only the athlete's *conscious mind* instead of reaching to the roots of the problem deep in the athlete's *body* and brain.

The athlete struggling in the clutches of an RSPP experiences overwhelmingly high levels of anxiety as he or she approaches the problematic action. The pitcher with control problems, the catcher who can't throw the ball back to the pitcher, the gymnast about to attempt her back handspring on beam, the soccer goalie who bobbles the ball under pressure, and the golfer over a three-foot putt are all preoccupied by the thought, *What if it happens again?* The athlete, trapped in anticipatory anxiety, repeatedly plays out this self-fulfilling prophecy. Consequently, the athlete ends up with that deer-in-the-headlights look.

The athlete is then unknowingly in a primordial state of fear no different than that of our mammalian ancestors. The core of these RSPPs can be understood by examining the universal, involuntary survival mechanisms wired into all animals: *the fight/flight response.* Sensing danger, all animals respond with neurophysiological changes that prepare them for the perceived threat by either fighting back or escaping in flight. All available energy is channeled into survival as adrenaline increases heart rate and respiration, tightens muscles, and slows digestion.

Predator and prey

This instinctual danger response is appropriate when confronted by a real threat but wreaks havoc when it emerges during a performance. This biological stress response dramatically disrupts the athlete's ability to stay loose, calm, and focused, which is a critical prerequisite for expanded performance. What we call choking is actually the fight/flight response acting out of time and place.

It is not widely known that another part of our survival mechanism is even more responsible for fueling RSPPs. This part is the *freeze* response described by Peter Levine in his book *Waking the Tiger—Healing Trauma.* When confronted by a predator, a prey animal immediately goes into the fight/flight instinct. When these survival options are not possible and the prey has been caught, it falls into the reptilian instinct of total immobility, or freeze. This response serves two purposes. First, freezing is a last-ditch survival attempt, as many predators will not eat prey that they perceive as dead. Second, by freezing, the animal enters an altered state in which pain isn't felt, ensuring that it won't suffer if it is devoured.

If the predator loses interest in its "dead" prey and wanders off, the prey animal literally *shakes off* the residual effects of this freeze state and regains active control of its body. It then returns to the wild and resumes its life, unaffected by this brush with death. Shaking free from the traumatic experience allows the animal to fully discharge the frozen energy that was mobilized for survival.

Humans, unlike our animal progenitors, don't naturally recover from this traumatic freeze. Although we reflexively slip into freeze, we have lost much of our ability to discharge it. This physical and emotional residue leads to trauma symptoms like panic, helplessness, flashbacks, dissociation, and avoidance. All of these symptoms are clearly visible in the athlete struggling with an RSPP.

Until David Grand's discoveries of the trauma basis of RSPPs, the crippling effects of the freeze response in athletes were mysteriously unresolvable. Although athletes are rarely exposed to life-threatening situations, their high-stakes challenges often trigger the fight/flight/freeze response. Success comes to the less traumatized, but panic, blocking, and failure come to the more traumatized: the gymnast on the beam can't go backwards, the diver is frozen on the board, the golfer freezes over a crucial putt, and the pitcher with the bases loaded death-grips the ball.

Unlike the symptom-focused approach of traditional sports psychology, Brainspotting Sports Work identifies and targets performance problems stuck in the athlete's brain and body, down to the roots of the

RSPP. This is accomplished by the holistic, brain-body–centered approach, the foundation of this book, which utilizes Brainspotting Sports Work (featured in Chapters 9 and 10), pioneered by Dr. Grand. This method makes use of left-right brain activation with moving sound in addition to a process that locates and releases trauma by eye position, all helping the athlete "process through" the underlying traumas feeding his or her performance difficulties. Brainspotting Sports Work once and for all releases the physical and emotional baggage that has silently accumulated over the years, freeing the athlete to return to top form and to go beyond.

This is your Brain on Sports: Beating Blocks, Slumps and Performance Anxiety for Good! provides a breakthrough perspective on the mystery of RSPPs. We provide the blocked athlete and his or her coaches and parents with essential information about the genesis of RSPPs, how they are misunderstood and mistreated, and the concrete steps for providing resolution and return to optimal performance. This book educates coaches and parents as to how to best understand and interact with the struggling athlete so as to become part of the solution rather than part of the problem. In addition, our book goes beyond problem solving and slump busting to help expand the athlete's performance to new heights.

Chapter 1 opens our discussion of RSPPs by telling Mackey Sasser's story. As mentioned earlier, his promising Major League career was abruptly cut short by the throwing yips, a mysterious malady that resisted the best efforts of more than 50 experts. Mackey's problem clearly illustrates the nature and origins of RSPPs and introduces our revolutionary theory that repetitive performance problems derive from underlying trauma. We illustrate how unless these wounds are addressed at the core, the athlete can't regain top form. Our sessions with Mackey reveal Brainspotting Sports Work, which remarkably healed his still active yips some 11 years after his career had ended.

Chapter 2, "The Body Keeps the Scorecard," details how injuries and traumas unconsciously accumulate in the athlete's brain and body and develop into RSPPs. Unlike normal experiences, which is naturally processed to completion and stored in the deep recesses of the brain, physical and emotional traumas remain unprocessed, frozen in their entirety. Months and years later, when exposed to a situation reminiscent of the original event, the vulnerable athlete experiences flashbacks, panic, avoidance, and other confusing trauma symptoms that generate anxiety and undermine performance. We have labeled this phenomenon sports traumatic stress disorder (STSD). We have also observed athletes exhibiting the more extreme symptoms found in the clinical condition called dissociation, including blanking out, body numbness, loss of function, feeling strange, or leaving their bodies.

Chapter 3, "The Fight/Flight/Freeze Response," outlines the body's built-in survival mechanism, the fight/flight/freeze response that contributes to repetitive performance problems. We give special attention to the overlooked freeze response that occurs in the wild when prey animals can't escape their predators. This same freeze is seen on the field when the panicked athlete locks up and can't perform. Athletes' yips can finally be understood when put in the context of these freeze instincts.

Chapter 4, "Calder's Story," tells of a gifted pitcher who, as a college freshman, suddenly developed severe control problems. Calder's yips threatened to derail his college career and his lifelong dream of playing pro ball. His story is instructive, as it graphically illustrates the development process of RSPPs and their relationship to sports injuries and emotional traumas tracing back to early childhood. Calder's story is also unique because it entails long-term treatment of several years and highlights the profound impact that Brainspotting Sports Work has on the athlete's life *outside of sports*.

Chapter 5, "Repetitive Sports Performance Problems and the Athlete as a Person," focuses on the need to recognize the athlete as a person separate from his or her performance. Coaches, parents, and sports psychologists often focus on "fixing" the athlete's problem and in the process neglect the athlete as a person with unique sensitivities, feelings, and needs. We show that the performance problem can't be healed without also healing the athlete as an entire person. This person-centered approach is illustrated with the story of an equestrian struggling with an RSPP spanning 35 years.

Chapter 6, "Amanda's Story," examines the return to form of a 12-year-old level-9 gymnast paralyzed by fear following a serious accident on the uneven bars. Amanda was the first gymnast that I observed healed by the power of Brainspotting Sports Work. Her story powerfully reveals the limitations of traditional sports psychology in resolving trauma-based performance problems. Amanda's intense fears illustrate the ineffectiveness of techniques such as positive self-talk, mental rehearsal, relaxation, and other mental-toughness strategies, which I initially tried with her unsuccessfully.

Chapter 7, "Whose Sport Is This Anyway?" discusses the destructive power that athlete, coach, and parent expectations have on performance and how they feed RSPPs. Expectations are outcome-related and attach an overinflated importance to a particular performance. As a consequence, they create an internal crisis for the athlete to perform up to certain standards. The athlete experiences the crisis as an inner sense of emergency, ("I have to…I've got to…I must….Oh, no. What if I don't?"). This internal urgency tightens the athlete's muscles, inhibits fluidity of motion, undermines self-confidence, and distracts concentration from the task at hand. The pressure of expectations consistently shuts down an athlete's performance and worsens RSPPs.

Chapter 8, "Self-talk and Repetitive Sports Performance Problems," reveals why positive self-talk, a staple of traditional sports psychology, is essentially ineffective in combating repetitive performance problems. We show how the thinking and talking areas of the brain cannot reach or affect the deep survival areas of the brain that hold the RSPPs. As the frightened, blocked athlete performs, no amount of positive self-talk or logical reasoning can override his or her activated fight/flight/freeze response.

Chapter 9 outlines step-by-step the treatment process and techniques used in Brainspotting Sports Work. We reveal how and why we have consistently achieved unprecedented results in every sport, describing in detail our groundbreaking sports-psychology model. This work has the remarkable capacity to explore past physical and emotional traumas while staying grounded in the present. The brain and the body are harnessed to do the work on their own, thus eliminating the time-consuming and inefficient rehashing of the past found in traditional talk therapy. We illustrate the state-of-the-art Brainspotting Sports Work tools that directly target the brain and body, locating and releasing the frozen traumas that knock the athlete off of his or her game. We also show how these same techniques can help to the blocked athlete soar to heights beyond his or her imagination.

Chapter 10, "Self-Help for Repetitive Sports Performance Problems," explains how the athlete can use our powerful tools on his or her own. Here we outline in detail what the athlete can do at home to address the anxiety, self-doubt, and frustration related to his or her blocked performance. We also explain exercises the athlete can use directly on the field to help relax and increase concentration. These carefully developed exercises have proven highly successful for the numerous athletes we have worked with. Step by step, athletes will be able to free themselves from what holds them back and learn how to mentally prepare themselves for the game from their deep brain and body, the source of their greatest performances.

This Is Your Brain On Sports: Beating Blocks, Slumps and Performance Anxiety for Good! is a truly revolutionary book that will change the face of sports psychology and influence performance work beyond the sports world. It reveals the groundbreaking notion that all repetitive performance problems come from physical and emotional traumas held in the brain and body in what we call STSD. First, the athlete has to know how to find the trauma, and then he or she has to know how to release it. We not only hold these keys, which we have used to help so many amazed, grateful athletes, but also share them with you right here on these pages. We hope you enjoy the ride.

CHAPTER 1

MACKEY SASSER, NEW YORK METS CATCHER
The Anatomy of a Repetitive Sports Performance
Problem (RSPP)

I (DG) have been a New York Mets fan since the team was first formed in 1962. I went to games at the old Polo Grounds that first year and excitedly watched the construction of Shea Stadium soon after. I was even there when they were laying down the sod for the brand-new infield. When the '69 Mets won the championship, it was one of the highlights of my adolescence. I distinctly remember when the Mets acquired catcher Mackey Sasser from the Pittsburgh Pirates. Sasser was brought in because Gary Carter, the aging Mets catcher, was injury ridden and the Mets needed more depth behind the plate. Although I believed that no one could really fill Carter's shoes, I was hopeful that the affable Sasser could get the job done. The 6'1", 210-pound catcher was an aggressive hitter and surprisingly agile for a big man. He had a strong arm and a quick release down to second.

In his rookie season, the hard-hitting Sasser batted .285 and had an on-base percentage of .313. His numbers continued to steadily improve, and in 1990, Mackey hit .307 and looked to be the catcher of the future for the New York franchise. The post-Gary Carter era seemed to be well under way, and I was encouraged.

Despite Sasser's considerable abilities both behind the plate and at bat, however, all was not right with the catcher. In his rookie year with the Mets, Mackey occasionally struggled with the seemingly simple task of throwing the ball back to the pitcher. Sasser would sometimes double,

Mackey Sasser at bat

triple, and even quadruple pump the ball before releasing it. When he did finally let go of the ball, his throw was more often a soft flip rather than a hard throw. Curiously, Mackey had absolutely no problem nailing a runner trying to steal second. After a while, opposing runners took advantage of this pre-throw idiosyncrasy, timing their delayed steals to Sasser's pumping motions.

Mackey's throwing problem emerged before I became an expert on performance and trauma work. Back then I was like most people who assumed that Mackey's difficulties would go away on their own. As a baseball fan I was aware of how Pirates' pitcher Steve Blass had completely lost his control 15 years earlier. What made Mackey's situation so confusing was the fact that initially, Sasser could throw effectively in the bullpen and to second base. He just couldn't get the ball back to the pitcher *during* the game. At the time it made no sense at all. Little did I know that 16 years later I would be working with Mackey on this very same issue.

In 1990, his best hitting year in the majors, Sasser's throwing difficulties worsened. The New York fans and media responded with cruelty. "Sasser syndrome" had hit the Big Apple. "Sasser's Throwing His Career Away," headlined the sports pages. Sasser was the butt of innumerable jokes, and during games, the hometown fans loudly counted in unison, "One, two, three," as Mackey pumped the ball. His throwing paralysis and its accompanying embarrassment became so intense that Sasser had panic attacks every night before a game.

That same year, Sasser was run over by the Braves' Jim Pressley in a hard collision at home plate. Mackey badly sprained his right ankle and partially tore his Achilles tendon and was out for six weeks. When he returned to the team, he was never the same ball player. His hitting dropped off, and his throwing problems worsened to the point that he couldn't get the ball to leave his hand. He saw increasingly less action behind the plate and ultimately was released in November of 1992. I was truly sad to see him go, but I was pleased for Mackey when he was quickly signed by the Mariners. In the early part of his second year with Seattle, Mackey's throwing problem was back in full force and he was taken out of the defensive lineup. In 1995, after brief stints with the Padres and Pirates, Sasser retired. He returned home to Alabama to coach baseball at his alma mater, Wallace Community College.

Around the time that Mackey left the Mets, I began doing more and more work as a psychotherapist in the area of trauma. As a clinician, I had been learning and developing new tools like EMDR (eye movement desensitization and reprocessing) and SE (somatic experiencing) and was surprised and delighted to see how much healing I was able to bring to trauma survivors. These new tools and technology even helped my clients work through traumas that they hadn't initially reported to me. This kind of work oriented me more toward the body and its role in controlling emotions and affecting behavior. I observed how **people who had been in accidents or had been injured physically carried these traumas both in their bodies and brains long after the events were over**. It was as if trauma left dual imprints on both the mind and body and that the two were inexorably linked together.

I quickly recognized the possibility of applying what I learned from these observations to athletes like Mackey who were, as a natural part of playing their sport, so prone to injuries. I thought, *If trauma leaves a physical and emotional imprint on the athlete, could it be that this imprint is causing these repetitive performance problems?* The more I saw how golfers, pitchers, catchers, skaters, and gymnasts got so easily entangled performance-wise, the more I wondered about the potential trauma basis to these problems. It made me think back to Mackey and his throwing woes. I wondered what would have happened if I'd had the skills and opportunity to work with him back when he was still in the majors.

Throughout his entire ordeal, Mackey desperately wanted to solve his problem but was completely helpless to do so. He was clueless as to why he couldn't make this pressure-less throw back to the pitcher without hesitating. **How was it possible that in a sport where he had excelled, being MVP at every level he played, he suddenly was unable to execute the simplest of skills?** In a desperate attempt to find a solution, Mackey saw so many psychologists and experts that he almost lost count. He even worked with a hypnotist, but nothing helped and the problem worsened.

When we met Mackey for the first time in the summer of 2006, 11 years after his playing career ended, he was still searching for answers. He claimed that **not a day went by** without someone asking him what had happened with his throwing. At our initial meeting, Mackey admitted there were times as a coach that he still struggled to throw batting practice. He was still having trouble releasing the ball without hesitating. In fact, it was the performance problem that now blocked him from coaching in the majors, a dream he still held, despite having left the game. "I could be a damn good bullpen coach in the bigs, but I'd have to throw batting practice. I'm afraid I couldn't cut it and face that humiliation again."

When we asked Mackey to tell us about his history and childhood, we were looking for both emotional traumas and physical injuries that might have unconsciously built up over the years, finally culminating in his throwing problem. *Mackey's personal and injury history clearly revealed what most "experts" had completely missed about his seemingly unusual throwing difficulty.*

RSPPs do not come out of the blue. They aren't something that can be "caught" from an infected teammate, and they have nothing to do with being a "head case." *They are the byproducts of the gradual accumulation within the athlete's brain and body of physical and emotional injuries over the course of the athlete's life and career. Period.* By the time the performance problem becomes visible to the athlete, coaches, and general public, most, if not all, of these earlier traumas have either long been forgotten or completely dismissed as having no significance, yet the athlete's body has not forgotten and in fact has been unconsciously keeping an exquisitely detailed scorecard of these injuries and their associated emotions.

The physical and emotional effects of the body's scorecard are what ultimately interfere with the athlete's natural talent, countless hours of training, and extensive experience. How is it possible for an athlete who was an MVP at every level to be unable to execute the most basic of skills? *The athlete's mind and body always hold the answer.*

Mackey Sasser's story clearly illuminates why traditional sports psychology is inadequate in explaining and ineffective in treating, those athletes who struggle with RSPPs. When you look more carefully at athletes' throwing problems and underlying injury histories using the lens of our paradigm, the mystery of Sasser Syndrome, Steve Blass Disease, and similar inexplicable performance problems across every sport begins to unravel. I (DG) worked with Mackey four times over the course of nine months. The initial session took place in Manhattan, New York, and lasted approximately five hours. The final session took

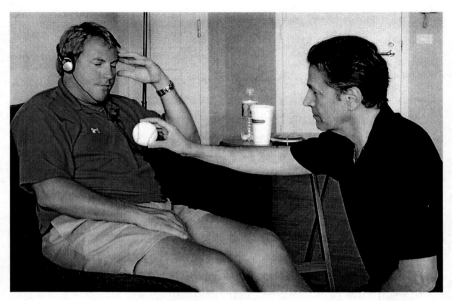

Mackey Sasser in session with Dr. Grand

place in Dothan, Alabama, and lasted 90 minutes. In between were two half-hour phone consultations.

Sasser had suffered a number of significant injuries during his high school, college, and professional career, and these silently formed the foundation of his performance block. In addition, he had experienced several earlier, profound non–sports-related traumas, and *all of these* contributed to the later emergence of his yips. It's notable that not one of the more than 50 professionals Mackey saw over the course of his career ever inquired about *any of these negative experiences* or their possible relationship to his then current throwing troubles.

As Mackey recalled his early childhood with me, he shared two pieces of his history right off the bat. The first was that his father suffered from a severe rheumatoid condition that significantly limited his activities, leaving him crippled with pain. It was impossible for his dad to throw overhand to Mackey when they first started playing catch when Mackey was three. Instead, his father flipped the ball underhanded to his young son. Mackey's father coped with his persistent pain by self-medicating with alcohol (he was described as a "quiet alcoholic"), and as a consequence, at a young age, Mackey took on a caretaker role in the family.

The second piece of personal history that Mackey shared was that at age seven, he witnessed his five- year-old brother run into the street and get hit by a car. The vehicle struck the boy in the chest and threw him 100 feet in the air. Mackey's brother was "dead at the scene," but the EMTs managed to revive him. According to Mackey, his brother was never the same physically or emotionally. Even though he was just seven, Mackey was wracked by guilt that he had failed in his responsibility to watch over his brother.

It struck me (DG) how a seven-year-old boy must have felt watching this horrific scene unfold as he was *frozen in fear and helplessness in his mind and body*. His helplessness must have only intensified when his shocked parents arrived at the accident scene and he witnessed their agony. This theme of helplessness seemed to play out over and over again both on and off the playing field as Mackey recalled the other details of his personal history. When he was 14, his dad's best friend and business partner was murdered during a robbery just moments *after* Mackey left the shop. Apparently, the murderer, whom Mackey had known, had been waiting for the boy to leave. This tragic incident seemed to emotionally take the wind out of his father's sails, and the man subsequently gave up on life. Mackey again felt the weight of responsibility for both the event and the impact that it had on his father.

At 10 years old, Mackey fell 15 feet from a tree, landing on the rusty edge of a 55-gallon drum. Multiple stitches closed the deep wounds on his chin and leg, yet 34years later, he winced in pain recalling the incident. At 12, Mackey had a Baker's cyst surgically removed from his left knee. At 17, he tore ligaments in the same knee while sliding into second base, requiring more surgery. Knees are critical equipment to a catcher, central to squatting and throwing. Knee injuries requiring surgery expose the athlete to more trauma. The body is *always* traumatized by surgery, even when it is necessary and helpful. Along with sports injuries and emotional traumas, surgeries are etched into the body's exquisitely detailed scorecard, and they become part of the body's cumulative storehouse that unconsciously fuels later performance problems.

Getting blindsided is a sports trauma

Mackey played quarterback in high school and was often hit while releasing the football. At 18, he played quarterback in a semi-pro league against older, larger players. On one play while backpedaling, Mackey was blindsided in the ribs. The hard hit eluded his protective padding, leaving him sore for weeks. Although the soreness disappeared, however, his body never forgot. It's interesting to note that the body mechanics of throwing a baseball and a football are basically the same. A righty turns sideways and lines up his left arm in the direction of the target. He then rocks back and shifts his weight to his right foot as he cocks his arm. His weight then shifts forward as he releases and follows through. This exposes a right-handed quarterback's left flank to hits from the onrushing defense.

Mackey's body and mind exquisitely remembered the details of this blindsiding, especially his body movement the moment he was hit. Whenever back in this position, throwing a pass or tossing a baseball back to the pitcher, the details of Mackey's trauma, unconsciously stored in his brain and body, were activated into his consciousness. As his body remembered, he felt fear and body tightness as he reared back

to throw. *This fear and physical tension were what impeded his quick, accurate, and smooth execution of a throw.*

In 1984, Mackey was drafted by the San Francisco Giants. That year, Sasser again hurt his knee while sliding, requiring surgical repair of torn cartilage. Over the course of his career, Mackey had the same knee operated on, repeatedly cleaning out bone chips.

In 1985 in AA ball in the Texas League, Mackey was run over at the plate by Kevin Keene, who kneed him in the head during the collision. Mackey suffered from whiplash and a possible concussion. The right side of his body and neck were too sore for him to play for several days.

Although all these injuries and traumas predated the emergence of Sasser's unique throwing problem, they all unconsciously contributed to it. Just as muscle memory develops through countless repetitions over time, *it also records the collective injuries.* Movements that *approximate* those involved in the original injury call up anxiety and muscle tension.

The first signs of Sasser's throwing yips came in 1987 in Calgary early in the season. It was a cold night, and Sasser caught a hard foul tip in the seam between the catcher's protection. A jolt of pain shot through his right shoulder and traveled down his throwing arm. Against his better judgment, Mackey stayed in the game as his shoulder progressively stiffened. In pain, he couldn't pull his arm back to cock the ball before the throw, so Mackey began keeping his arm tucked in close to his body like a bird with a broken wing. The only way he could toss the ball back to the pitcher was to flip it off of his fingertips. He continued this for a few games, but when his shoulder finally felt better, he couldn't regain his normal throwing motion.

After returning to San Francisco, Mackey continued to struggle. Soon, he was confronted by a coach who made a spectacle of his throwing difficulties. The coach told Mackey, and all his teammates in earshot, that he was fining Sasser $20 every time he hesitated in his throw. Although the coach thought "tough love" would help, drawing attention to Mackey's problem only intensified it. The result of this increased self-consciousness was predictable: Sasser's throwing problem worsened.

Mackey's experience with his coach highlights a common dynamic for athletes struggling with RSPPs. *The performance problem is cyclical; the trauma(s) lead to symptoms, which ultimately causes additional trauma for the athlete. Embarrassment and humiliation by coaches, parents, and fans always has a traumatic effect on the athlete.* The cruelty, insensitivity, and humiliation that the athlete endures make the performance difficulty more severe and intractable. The added anxiety further tightens muscles, distracts the athlete, and ensures that the performance difficulty will continue and worsen.

Coaches can help or hurt

Later in 1987, after Sasser was traded to the Pirates, his problems with his left knee reemerged. Team trainers thought that the bulge on the outside of Mackey's left knee was another Baker's cyst and repeatedly needled it, attempting to drain it, but *the bulge was actually a torn muscle* that later required another surgery.

In 1990, Mackey was having a great year before he tore his Achilles tendon in a hard collision at home plate with Atlanta's Jim Pressley. Mackey was out for six weeks. The collision also damaged Mackey's left side so he couldn't rock back when he threw, so when he returned to action, his throwing problem was more pronounced. He described a "fog of anxiety" rolling over him when he thought about throwing. Frequently, he couldn't get the ball to leave his hands. In this same year, Mackey's father succumbed to cancer.

In 1994, Sasser was traded to Seattle. In the second game of spring training, Kevin Ryan collided hard with him at the plate, breaking Mackey's left scapula. His trainer thought that Sasser's shoulder was dislocated and attempted to jam the shoulder back into place. Of course, this misdiagnosis and ill-directed treatment caused Mackey more trauma. According to Sasser, this injury was the "nail in the coffin" to his career; within a year, he was out of Major League Baseball for good.

Mackey Sasser's bizarre throwing problem and its connection to his personal and injury histories point out another crucial concept regarding the mystery of RSPPs: ***RSPPs are always intricately connected to the athlete's personal history***. Traditional sports psychology tends to have a myopic perspective with athletes. Over-focusing on solving the performance problem leads to ignoring the athlete as a unique individual. Early experiences that have significantly affected the athlete's life and personality aren't deemed relevant to the performance problem in the present. Why didn't the 50 professionals who worked with Sasser ever ask him about his life history and the innumerable physical injuries that shaped his career as an athlete? ***We believe that one should never separate an athlete's performance problem from who he or she is as a unique human being.*** That, of course, includes the individual's trauma history.

With post-traumatic stress disorder (PTSD), the individual continues to relive or *associate* to the traumatic experience. Present-day sights, sounds, or interactions trigger old memories. The individual then responds *as if* he is reliving the trauma in the current moment. He may feel the same emotions and the same physical sensations and even think the same thoughts he did in the original experience.

Sports traumatic stress disorder (STSD) is a subtler form of the condition. Most often, the afflicted athlete *is unaware of the connection* between his performance difficulties and past traumatic experiences but is acutely aware of the anxiety, body tension, and negative thinking embedded in the performance problem. Mackey was flooded with anxiety, dread, and negative thinking whenever he was about to throw in games, but he had absolutely no awareness of the experiences that were fueling his panic and block.

The information from Mackey's history guided us in unraveling the mystery of his long-standing throwing yips. As we will discuss in more detail in Chapter 9, our model targets the accumulated frozen traumas held in the athlete's brain and body. We use a combination of neurophysiological techniques (developed by myself) that help locate, focus, and release frozen accumulated traumas. The main approach, called Brainspotting, works by finding the eye position that coordinates with where the trauma is held in the brain. By gazing at a pointer in this eye position, the brain and body process and release the trauma, sometimes with remarkable speed. Brainspotting is made *even more* effective with bilateral brain stimulation from BioLateral CDs with nature sounds and healing music panning back and forth between left and right ears.

Brainspotting helps unfreeze the frozen traumatic experiences from the past so they can be fully processed through in the present. Old traumas lose their connections in the brain and body and their power to express themselves in fears and blocks. As a result, athletes' anxieties dissipate and they feel freed up enough to perform "like their own selves."

This is how my work went with Mackey during our initial face-to-face marathon. We started by targeting two of the traumatic experiences from early in his life: watching his brother get hit by a car, and falling out of a tree onto a rusted oil drum. Our aim is for the athlete to work things through until there is absolutely no reaction when the incident is called to consciousness.

After Brainspotting the first two traumas to a point of completion, we focused on Mackey's childhood sadness over his dad's debilitating rheumatoid arthritis. Sasser brought up the still-vivid image of his father's inability to even flip a ball back to him overhand. His first thought struck like lightning: "I'm talking about my dad being unable to throw, and here I am having these same problems." When this trauma was healed, we began to systematically address Mackey's long list of sports injuries. We were both surprised at how the healing cascaded forward like falling dominos. Mackey's processing jumped around chronologically as old emotions and physical feelings reemerged randomly. One profound flash was from Seattle, just before he left baseball for good, when he couldn't release the ball without pumping three or four times on *every* throw. Sasser reexperienced his humiliation and self-contempt. He remembered thinking, *Please don't put me in there (catching). I don't want the failure and embarrassment.*

After processing all of that through, Mackey saw "flipping images" of being blindsided as he stepped up to throw a pass, countless collisions at home plate, being knocked down and bowled over by runners, catching endless foul tips on various parts of his body, and the numerous surgeries throughout his life. As we fully processed through each of these experiences, Mackey began to deeply understand how all these events had culminated in his throwing yips.

When even more targeted work was necessary, I encouraged Mackey to further activate specific traumas by physically reenacting the movements in extreme slow motion. Whenever Sasser reported an upsurge in distress, I had him stop and hold the position he was in. This technique helps call up any residual physical sensations or emotions. For full release, I also "invented" a new application of this technique for Mackey. I guided him to recall the injury he sustained in Calgary in 1987 (when he caught the foul tip off the seam in his chest protector) that triggered the emergence of his throwing yips. Holding a baseball 10 feet away from Sasser, I moved the ball extremely slowly toward the site of the impact. As I moved the ball progressively closer to his shoulder, his distress spiked. I held the ball in place (for instance, five feet away) until all the distress had dispersed. Then I moved it closer until the next spike(say, three feet away). I was amazed by how much trauma was left after all the focused work we had done, so we continued this procedure until Mackey comfortably observed the ball move closer and closer. Eventually, I was able touch the point of impact with the ball *with no activation for Mackey at all*.

We also use micro-movement to locate and release traumas that did not emerge in our injury history-taking process. For example, with a throwing block like Mackey's, we have the athlete reenact the entire motion extremely slowly. As he does so, we look for minute releases of physical or emotional tension (jerks, jumps, or twitches), which disrupt the smooth motion and execution. We also ask the athlete to indicate any posi-

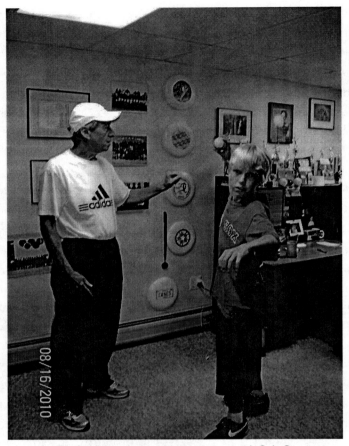

Dr. Goldberg doing micro movement with Cole S.

tion that activates distress. We then guide the athlete to hold the physical pose and observe whatever comes up. These minute disruptions reveal where hidden traumas have been stored. Accordingly, our micro-movement technique finds and releases the traumas.

When we finished this initial extended session, Mackey reported feeling both exhausted and relaxed. Although he didn't get a chance to do much throwing immediately afterward, he reported that he felt significantly calmer in his daily life. Over the course of the next eight months, I had two 30-minute follow-up phone sessions with him, and he reported feeling more relaxed and comfortable with himself. ***This sense of ease also translated into improved capacity to throw batting practice. He no*** *longer experienced any anxiety or tension when he threw and was able to release the ball smoothly and accurately.*

Nine months after our initial meeting with Sasser, we traveled down to Dothan, Alabama, to meet directly with Mackey again. *The previous day, he had thrown batting practice for an hour without hesitation or anxiety. Mackey's throwing yips were completely gone.* As he put it, "Everything has been upbeat since we first met. I found out a lot of things about myself and kind of played off that. I feel calmer and more relaxed. Batting practice has been good. I'm throwing the ball well and not having any problems at all. I can pick up a ball and just throw it right away, where I used to be afraid when there was a big crowd around watching. I don't have that fear now. *It's gotten to the point where I really don't think about throwing. It just feels good, and I can locate the ball where I want.*"

In Chapter 2, we will closely detail how injuries and traumas unconsciously accumulate in the athlete's brain and body and later emerge as RSPPs. Unlike normal experiences that are naturally processed to completion and stored in the deep recesses of the brain, physical and emotional traumas remain unprocessed, and it's these frozen remnants that, left untreated, fuel the athlete's anxiety, body tension, and disrupted concentration that are so characteristic of RSPPs.

CHAPTER 2

THE BODY KEEPS THE SCORECARD
Sports Injuries and the Roots of Repetitive Sports
Performance Problems

Colin Burns was a skilled Division I goalkeeper referred to me (AG) in his junior year because excessive pregame nervousness undermined his confidence. Before games he was preoccupied with fear of making mistakes, which left him feeling like "a total wreck." During games he ruminated about everything that could go wrong in goal, leaving him incapacitated by anxiety. He hoped the ball wouldn't venture to his side of the field, a mindset that was clearly not conducive to expanded performance. When facing opponent attack, he was tentative, indecisive, and ineffective. His subpar play rarely reflected his high-level skills and extensive experience and training. Because of inconsistency between the posts, Colin suffered further humiliation, losing his starting slot to a less talented *freshman*.

Most puzzling were Colin's complaints of extreme discomfort handling shots coming ***directly*** at him, especially his face, as he had no problem diving wide left or right for balls. Neither shots high above him or low at his feet caused him problems, but whenever a shot veered toward his head, he panicked, froze, and misplayed the ball.

Colin dreamed of playing soccer at higher levels, but his nervousness, poor play, and demotion challenged his hopes of attaining this goal. Despite losing the faith of his coaches and teammates, he somehow refused to give up on himself. And occasionally, he rebounded and played fearlessly and brilliantly. He maintained the belief that somehow, he could overcome his fear and live up to his potential.

Colin Burns, goalie of Swedish team, Ljungskile

Colin's and Mackey's cases, along with our other stories, illustrate the revolutionary paradigm shift presented in this book: ***The roots of all significant performance problems are in the athlete's sports trauma history, especially in sports injuries, which are simultaneous physical and emotional traumas.*** Frequently, these physical traumas, often sports related, are suffered in childhood and adolescence and unconsciously accumulate over time. Occasionally, these injuries can be directly related to the performance problem, having occurred a few months to a year before their emergence, but usually, the connection is unseen because the negative experiences may have occurred years before the performance problem emerged.

In referencing the word *trauma*, we are not using the narrow definition of life-threatening events such as violent assaults, childhood abuse, serious car accidents, war, and natural disasters. At times, these events do underlie and contribute to an athlete's performance problems. The term *sports trauma* or the negative experiences we refer to can be as innocuous as a near miss for the athlete, with no physical injury occurring; these events can also be sprains, concussions, torn ligaments, broken bones, bad bruises, cuts, collisions, or even witnessing the injury of another athlete. We have repeatedly observed that the traumatic nature of any experience is *determined by the meaning that is assigned to it by the individual him- or herself.*

Frequently, these negative experiences hold a strong emotional charge, which increases the athlete's struggles. Occasionally, they involve exposure to embarrassment and humiliation. ***The unconscious accumulation of these physical and emotional traumas in the athlete's brain and body are the root cause of all significant performance problems.*** The anxiety, loss of confidence, tentativeness, and body tension consciously experienced by the athlete are simply ***symptoms*** of these unconsciously accumulated, upsetting, negative experiences.

Like most goal keepers, Colin's trauma history was extensive, including numerous physically and emotionally traumatic negative events. For example, as a scrawny, 5'6", 145-pound high school freshman, he witnessed the starting keeper, a 6'2", 215-pound senior, getting kicked in the head and knocked unconscious. The head injury was so severe that it landed the starter in the ICU for a week and sidelined him for half the season. Visiting his teammate in the hospital, Colin was shaken to see the extent of this large, strong senior's injury. A week later, Colin started his first game, terrified that the same fate awaited him. On the first play in which he came

out of the goal, Colin caught an elbow to his head and sustained a concussion, the first of many in his career.

As a sophomore, Colin broke several bones in his right hand after being kicked while trying to stop a shot. As a junior he broke several toes in another collision. The summer before starting college, playing club ball, Colin sustained the most

Colin Burns making save

serious injury of his career. He came out of the net and dove for the ball as a defender attempted to kick it into the goal. Colin took a knee in the face, which broke his nose and the orbital bone around his right eye. Colin needed facial reconstruction surgery and was told by the doctor that he had come quite close to sustaining permanent brain damage.

Throughout his early soccer career, Colin received significant emotional abuse from a few coaches, undermining his self-confidence. He was scapegoated by his high school coach, whom Colin described as an angry, abusive man who screamed in tirades to "teach" his players the game. The coach had a few "chosen" athletes, and Colin was one of his favorite targets to humiliate in front of teammates and fans. Colin was blamed for every goal he allowed, even if the defense broke down in front of him and he had no chance at the save. As a junior in high school, Colin's club coach publicly berated him after a tough loss, calling Colin "the worst goal keeper in the state!" The emotional exposure from this kind of repeated coaching abuse understandably left Colin afraid of making mistakes.

Sports injury/sports trauma

In addition to the soccer injuries, Colin experienced an earlier injury that contributed to his performance difficulties. While Colin was bike racing at age seven, his front tire suddenly locked and he flew over his handlebars and landed face first on the cement. This memory was so vivid that 14 years later, he still remembered the taste of the cement and the pain in his teeth.

How do these kinds of physical and emotional injuries form the underpinnings of a present-day performance problem? What is there to link to an athlete's present-day anxiety, tight muscles, low self-confidence, and tentativeness as he or she performs?

When an athlete sustains a physical injury, a combination of physical and emotional aspects attach to this negative experience. The physical components are usually more obvious than the emotional ones and include the pain from sprains, bruises, muscle pulls, tendon and ligament tears, bone dislocations or breaks, concussions, and the physical effects of extended or serious illnesses like chronic fatigue syndrome, mononucleosis, or other infectious diseases.

It's also common for the athlete to experience additional physical and emotional trauma from the medical treatment of these injuries and illnesses, as in the pain and emotional discomfort that accompany surgery, getting stitches, having bones set, taking medications with unexpected side effects, enduring painful rehab, and unexpected complications to healing.

The emotional part of a physical trauma can include embarrassment over the injury, panic, helplessness, rage, depression, and intense feelings of loss. This includes the extreme frustration that the injury will keep the athlete out of training and competition for an extended time and includes the trauma *immediately* following an injury preceding medical intervention, when the athlete is uncertain about the extent and consequences of the physical damage. Before the coaches, trainers, or doctors reach the athlete, he or she is left with the immediate pain, physical appearance of the injury, and only the imagination of what has just happened and how bad it actually is. Remember, ***the traumatic nature of an event is always determined by the meaning that the individual ascribes to it.***

During the time before the medical intervention, which may be from several moments to a few days, the athlete's fearful imagination can wreak further emotional havoc on her, which can further fuel future performance difficulties. For example, a skier who takes a nasty fall and temporarily can't move may begin to ***think*** that she is paralyzed for life as she waits for help to arrive. When this notion is proven false minutes later, the emotional and physical impact on her mind and body are not erased.

The nature and extent of the trauma for the athlete is also affected by the attitude and response of both coaches and parents to the athlete's immediate injury. It is not unusual for an athlete to sustain a serious injury that isn't immediately visible. If the injury occurs in practice, the coach may either ignore or minimize the athlete's complaints. Too many coaches are guided by the machismo notion that if you're not bleeding or don't have a bone sticking through your skin, there's nothing wrong with you.

Diagram/Table #1
PHYSICAL & EMOTIONAL SOURCES OF TRAUMA

PHYSICAL SOURCES OF TRAUMA	EMOTIONAL SOURCES OF TRAUMA
Injuries	**Witnessing a serious injury**
sprains	fear and panic associated with injury
bruises	fear/panic of re-injury
muscle or ligament pulls	embarrassment/humiliation
muscle, ligament or tendon tears	feelings of helplessness
bone breaks or dislocations	intense feelings of loss
concussions	depression
long-term debilitating illness	loss of self-esteem and confidence
severe asthmatic reactions	self-image & identity confusion because of loss of sport
Treatment	frustration at not being able to train
surgery	imagination driven fear of what's wrong before accurate medical diagnosis
stitches	
unexpected complications of surgery resulting in additional medical intervention	shame/humiliation from coach's reaction to failure or performance problem
setting of broken bones	shame/humiliation from peer's/fan's reactions
negative side effects of and/or allergic reactions to medication	shame/humiliation from coach's reaction to athlete's injury
painful rehabilitation	parental empathic failure - when parents downplay or ignore the seriousness of an injury
unexpected complications of the healing processing	parental emotional abuse – when parents withdraw love after failure or performance problem
extended imobilization	

The physical and emotional causes of trauma

It's not unusual for this kind of coach to respond to the injured athlete in a demeaning way by challenging the athlete to "walk it off," "play through the pain," or "stop acting like a baby."

Although one might expect such an insensitive response in more macho sports like football, basketball, baseball, or hockey, this same coaching attitude is prevalent in gymnastics, where young female athletes may experience several falls as a routine part of *daily* practice. Some gymnastics coaches tend to doubt the veracity of a gymnast's complaints and often force her to continue practicing the skill that she may have just fallen on. Coercing an athlete to continue to perform while injured and fearful puts that athlete at an even greater risk of injury and further emotionally traumatizes her. Trust is a critical issue for the athlete who heavily relies on her coach for her safety.

At times, the athlete's parents, too caught up in their son or daughter's success in the sport, fail to pay enough attention to their child's physical complaints. Consequently, they may directly or indirectly pressure their child to continue to perform, especially if an important competition is coming up that the parents have become overly invested in. Even more so than the coach, the parents' job is to ensure that their child is safe both physically and emotionally. When parents forget this important role and coerce their child to continue to perform despite that child's injury complaints, these parents are further traumatizing their child. ***This kind of empathic failure underlies many of the most intractable performance problems that emerge later, sometimes in adulthood.***

These physical and emotional injuries ultimately form the foundation of the athlete's repetitive performance problem. Physical trauma generates a shock to the athlete's body integrity as well as to his sense of invincibility. For many athletes, the injury may be their first experience of their bodies failing them. Athletes pride themselves on their physicality, independence, and prowess, and the injury temporarily turns their world upside down, shattering their self-esteem and upsetting the psychological and emotional balance needed to cope and function at a high level.

To understand how this works, we can look at how the brain processes life experiences and stores memories. The brain, as the ultimate mind-body organ, has an innate tendency toward healing and recovery just like the body does. For example, when the body sustains a wound, it immediately takes steps to try to heal the wound by increasing blood flow to the site to flush out infection and begin clotting.

In parallel fashion, the brain attempts to always move toward a state of psychological equilibrium. Over the course of our lives, we are exposed to a variety of life experiences, some positive, some neutral, and some negative. Through a natural assimilation process, the brain adaptively processes these experiences so they are constructively integrated. What is useful from the experience is learned and stored in the brain with the appropriate emotion and is available for future use. When an experience is successfully assimilated or "digested," it is stored in the brain with little attached intense emotion or physical sensation. When we recall such an incident, we don't reexperience the old

Diagram/Table #2
HOW THE BRAIN PROCESSES AND STORES
"NORMAL" vs. TRAUMATIC EXPERIENCES

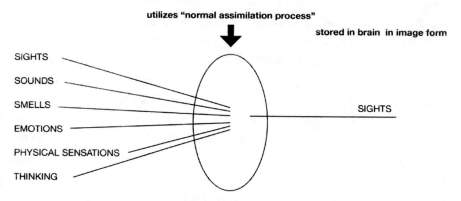

The brain storing "normal" vs. traumatic experiences

emotion or sensation with it. In this way we are ***informed by*** our past experiences and memories but not ***controlled*** by them, and with sports, our present athletic performances are not burdened by emotional or physical baggage from the past, only learned experience.

By contrast, ***trauma, or any strongly negatively charged experience, isn't adequately assimilated or processed. Instead, the upsetting incident remains stuck in the system in broken pieces.*** The body instantly memorizes the physical experience of the trauma in exquisite detail, including the body sensations of the impact and pain, along with the associated sights, sounds, smells, and tastes. The attached emotions and where they are felt in the body are frozen as well. The brain is overwhelmed, and instead of getting "digested," all of the information attached to the injury, including the negative thoughts, is stored in the brain *in exactly the same form it was initially experienced.*

Days, weeks, months, or even years later, when the athlete is in a situation reminiscent of the original trauma or experiences prolonged stress, the upsetting experience may be unconsciously activated, thus interfering with the performance of the moment. These components represent all of the sensory details from the earlier event that were frozen in the brain and body in their original disturbing state: the images, lighting, emotions, physical movements, sounds, or smells. These unique sensory details later returning to consciousness cause the performance-disrupting symptoms so common in RSPPs.

Colin, for example, always complained that his fear, anxiety, and lack of confidence were much more problematic when the weather was overcast and rainy. He claimed that there was something about the lighting and the slipperiness under foot in these game situations that he found unsettling. Upon closer examination, we discovered that these same overcast, rainy conditions had been present during two of Colin's more significant traumas. His brain and body had exquisitely memorized all of the details from both, including the weather, temperature, lighting, and footing. Whenever the details were duplicated in the pre-

Colin Burns between the posts

sent, Colin reexperienced the same intensity of anxiety originally associated with these frightening events. Colin's frozen memories tightened his muscles, undermined his confidence, and distracted his focus and concentration, making it impossible for him to perform to his potential.

The athlete usually has no conscious awareness of why he's experiencing these confusing and crippling feelings. All the athlete is aware of is that he's scared and can't relax and play his "normal" game. In his present experience, he may know that there is *no logical reason* to be feeling nervous and doubt-ridden. The problem is that his physical and emotional reactions, *being symptoms of the underlying trauma*, are completely out of his conscious control.

This is both extremely confusing and frustrating to the athlete and to those around him or her. The fact that one day she's performing effortlessly and the next day she's completely stuck baffles coaches and parents. They may first try to encourage the athlete to "just do it" and then later, out of frustration, use bullying tactics or even emotional abuse in an attempt to get her unstuck. Far too many coaches and parents fail to realize this very important fact: *The athlete mired in RSPPs has no conscious control over her performance problems and is often far more frustrated than the adults around her.*

The frustration of the athlete

It is precisely because of the unconscious roots of these RSPPs that the more conscious interventions of traditional sports-psychology techniques are ultimately ineffectual. These surface strategies like concentration training, thought-stopping, visualization, positive thinking, and relaxation fail to resolve the underlying source of the athlete's distress that are at the heart of the problem. Instead, these interventions are aimed at the conscious *symptoms* of the trauma base: the anxiety, self-doubts, and disrupted concentration. Quite often, however, the struggling athlete can't clearly articulate exactly what's bothering him or her. For example, a gymnast who was afraid of throwing her back handspring stood on the end of the beam with arms raised, ready to go, but could not get herself to throw it. Her breathing became rapid and shallow, and she went into a deer-in-the-headlights trance, with her body frozen. She stated that she didn't know what she was thinking about and had no idea where her concentration had gone. All she knew was that she was "freaking out" and couldn't get her body to go. She was unable to articulate what was actually going on because the problem was located outside of her conscious awareness, deep in her brain and body, where her past injuries and scary falls were stored.

In the past, I (AG) was always baffled by this kind of blank response from an athlete. I had always assumed, like most sports psychologists, that negative self-talk and faulty concentration were generating the fear and anxiety. I believed that if the self-talk and concentration mistakes were constructively changed, the problem would effectively resolve itself. When an athlete was unable to pinpoint what he was thinking about or focusing on, however, I felt at a loss as to how to help. Often I addressed these two performance variables, teaching the athlete how to both recognize and manage negative self-talk and to control focus and concentration, with little or no positive results. The athlete remained flooded with self-doubts and excessive nervousness and was unable to utilize any of the strategies that I had taught him.

I discovered later that *to conceptualize any athlete's problem using only the more traditional paradigm of commonly practiced sports psychology is to completely miss what's really going on*. I found that the athlete's negative self-talk, excessive nervousness and faulty focus are not directly *causing* her performance problems as sports psychologists believe. *Instead, they are in truth symptoms of the problem that may further contribute to and* **exacerbate the problem.**

Let us explain.

An athlete who suddenly and seemingly inexplicably finds himself unable to execute at his previous high level, struggling to do what used to be the routine for him, will have a predictable conscious reaction. Depending on the individual, this reaction may not always be in this exact order, but it will almost always entail certain elements. It's these elements and the negative performance-disrupting cycle they produce that then *further exacerbate* the athlete's performance woes.

At the initial signs of his problem, the athlete may begin to react with shock, dismay, and embarrassment. He is confused about why, suddenly and inexplicably, he is unable to get a hit, execute a dive or trick, make a short putt, or accurately throw a ball. Suddenly being unable to do something that used to be second nature brings humiliation to the experienced athlete. He responds to this initial shock and confusion by attempting to "fix" the problem. He begins to harness his energy, channeling it into his previously reliable, universal success strategy—"trying harder."

Most skilled athletes have achieved a high level of excellence because of their extraordinary work ethic and self-discipline. In the past, they have always been able to rely on these two traits to solve all of their performance problems. Utilizing this same focused "trying harder" strategy, the athlete begins to practice longer and with more intensity. The batter in a slump may take extra batting practice until his hands blister. A golfer with the putting yips may spend additional hours on the putting green every morning trying to get his stroke back. The catcher who has trouble accurately throwing the ball back to the pitcher may make 100 to 200 extra throws a day outside of organized practice in an attempt to fix things. As a consequence of all this added work, the athlete becomes even more preoccupied with the problem. Soon, he finds this preoccupation spreading to his life outside of the sport.

Unfortunately, the athlete's attempted solution of "trying harder" fails miserably because ***the problem is not a physical one. An athlete can never truly overcome an RSPP by physically practicing more.*** This "trying harder" approach is always doomed to fail and only adds to the athlete's growing frustrations. The athlete often turns to a coach or trainer to work on "correcting" his mechanics. Like trying harder, this approach also makes things worse. First, it gets the athlete over-thinking mechanics, which should be unconscious. Peak athletic performance is always controlled by our hind, non-thinking, brain, which processes information unconsciously. ***The more conscious and analytical an athlete gets about his or her performance, the more the athlete will struggle.*** Second, changing basic technique or mechanics in these situations is off the mark and usually further undermines the athlete's already shaky self-confidence.

Diagram/Table #3
THE SLUMP CYCLE

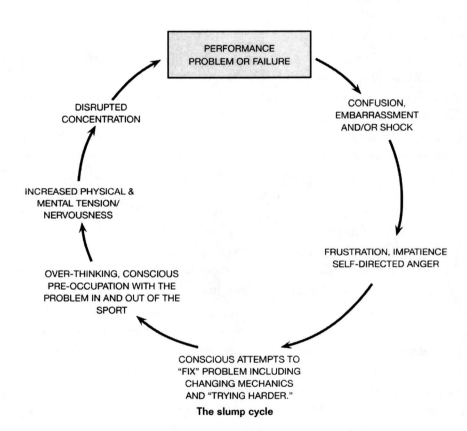

The slump cycle

As the athlete's best efforts to resolve the problem are continually met with failure, she becomes frustrated and angry with herself. This impatience and self-directed anger add more fuel to the fire, further tightening muscles and ensuring that the problem will worsen. Mounting frustration then leads the athlete to trying even harder, which results in more failure. ***This repetitive cycle of trying harder, failing, and then trying harder sends the athlete's performance spiraling downward.*** As the problem continues unabated and all attempts to fix it are met with repeated failure, the athlete's self-confidence is shaken to the core. As a result, she stops trusting herself and begins to seriously question her abilities.

As the athlete approaches practice and performance, dread and avoidance have replaced joy and excitement. He is overwhelmed by a preoccupation that "IT" will happen again. The resultant self-talk is primarily negative and fuels his doubts that he can ever make things right. As a result, his internal level of stress is high, tightening muscles and making smooth, relaxed execution impossible. As a consequence, his performances continue to suffer, further undermining his self-confidence, heightening his anxiety, and ensuring that his repetitive problems will continue. The athlete has found himself caught up in a vicious cycle that he is unknowingly maintaining.

Bobby, a Division I catcher who couldn't throw the ball back to the pitcher without either bouncing it in front of the pitcher or sailing it over the pitcher's head illustrates how a trauma-based performance problem is exacerbated by the athlete's conscious response to the symptoms of the trauma(s). Whenever Bobby attempted to make a routine, pressure-less throw back to the pitcher, his right thumb inexplicably tightened, making accurate throws impossible. Bobby's throwing yips started his sophomore year in high school in the next-to-last inning of a crucial playoff game in which he had performed flawlessly. Then, in the sixth inning, "something snapped upstairs" and suddenly he had a strange, anxious feeling in his body, throwing arm, and thumb. After he bounced three throws in front of the mound and sending one way over the pitcher's head, Bobby felt his anxiety become so intense that he couldn't finish the game. It didn't take very long for his problem and the attached anxiety to spread to any short throw, regardless of whether it was in a game or not.

Catchers can lose the ability to throw back to the pitcher

Bobby was at a loss to explain why, suddenly, he couldn't make these simple throws back to the pitcher. He had suffered no injuries in the game nor experienced any obvious incidents that might have triggered it, other than the intense pressure of the playoff game. In his sports history, however, Bobby had sustained numerous sports injuries, including several concussions from collisions at the plate, broken fingers on his throwing hand, a deep cut to his knee requiring 250 stitches, broken ribs from a football hit, and many emotionally upsetting experiences with humiliating coaches. These injuries and negative experiences silently formed the foundation of his throwing yips.

Bobby was humiliated by his sudden inability to perform these routine throws and, as expected, was preoccupied with what others thought of him. He wanted to play college ball and worried that his throwing problem would wreck his scholarship chances. On the field, he was hyperaware of the feelings in his throwing arm and thumb, and when he detected the slightest sensation of muscle tension there, he immediately panicked. Bobby began to dread having to play catcher and seriously considered changing positions to the outfield. Soon, his problems behind the plate began to affect his hitting, sending his batting average down the tubes.

Sports-psychology techniques aimed solely at his symptoms were ineffective in helping Bobby calm down and throw accurately. Despite learning several concentration and relaxation strategies, he couldn't effectively use them to relax and focus. No matter what he tried, he couldn't control the flood of negative self-talk or rising anxiety whenever he got behind the plate. He *knew* what he was supposed to think about and focus on, but he was unable to do either.

As a result, Bobby was paralyzed with fear that every time he'd attempt to throw, *"IT" would happen again*. This kind of anticipatory anxiety further exacerbated his yips.

It's important to understand that what Bobby was *really* struggling with was nothing more than the ***conscious symptoms of underlying trauma(s)***. The symptoms by themselves weren't *causing* the throwing difficulty; ***the real culprits were the old injuries that were being held outside of his awareness in his brain and body***. Under pressure, components of these past injuries (anxiety, muscle tension, negative thinking, and self-doubt) were unconsciously activated. These physical and emotional components then intruded into Bobby's present performance, causing his specific throwing problem. It wasn't until these past injuries were addressed and processed through (see Chapter 9) that he was finally able to relax enough to throw like his old self again.

The situation for any athlete struggling with RSPPs is complicated by additional negative experiences. Some of these events may be reminiscent of the original trauma—for example, sustaining a second or third concussion, breaking the same wrist twice, or being subjected to demeaning, humiliating behavior from another coach. At other times, these negative experiences may be very diverse and involve injuries to other parts of the body. As an athlete experiences these additional upsetting events, each of them is unconsciously stored in the brain and body in related memory networks. (A memory network is a series of channels in which related memories, thoughts, images, emotions, and sensations are stored and linked together.)

At any moment, any one or more of these unconsciously held channel memories can be activated and then flood the athlete's conscious experience with past images, emotions, sensations, and negative thinking. The athlete may be clueless that one or more negative experiences may be triggering him. Because of this, it's critical that ***all relevant negative experiences or traumas*** get fully processed through so the athlete is able to perform in the present without being weighed down by the baggage from the past.

This multiple-trauma effect is clearly illustrated in Colin's presenting problem of becoming visibly anxious whenever a ball was shot directly at his face. Every time Colin stepped between the posts, he was consciously and unconsciously returning to the scene of several accidents. Balls aimed at his face not only were a strong trigger for remembering those times that he had been kicked in the head or witnessed other keepers hurt in that way but also triggered his much earlier face-first bike accident. Much of the anxiety and dread that Colin experienced whenever he played in the present actually belonged to these unconsciously stored memories from the past.

Diagram/Table #4
MEMORY NETWORKS

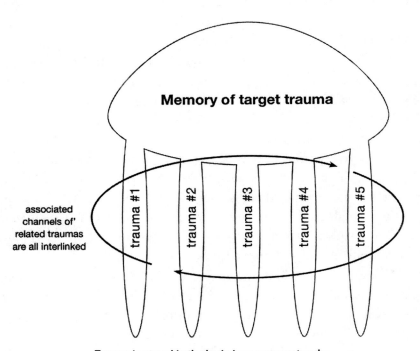

Memory of target trauma

associated
channels of'
related traumas
are all interlinked

trauma #1 trauma #2 trauma #3 trauma #4 trauma #5

Trauma is stored in the brain in memory networks

To sum up the major thesis of our model, *RSPPs* are initially cat-alyzed by the unconscious accumulation of past injuries and other negative experiences in the mind and body of the athlete. ***The hidden, silent physi-cal and emotional buildup from these past traumatic experiences are what ultimately contribute to the more visible symptoms that erupt in the cur-rent performance problem.*** Always complicating this picture is the athlete's unique reaction to his or her performance woes. The way an athlete responds to her performance difficulties frequently initiates a self-perpet-uating negative cycle that further undermines her self-confidence, gener-ates additional anxiety, and deepens the problem.

In the next chapter, we will explore how these past sports trau-mas and negative experiences interfere with expanded performance by triggering, outside of the athlete's awareness, the built-in survival mechanism that we share with all living creatures, the fight/flight/freeze response. It's our contention that most RSPPs are a direct result of this fight/flight/freeze response gone wrong. In fact, the vast majority of RSPPs are a reflection of an athlete helplessly and unknowingly stuck in the freeze part of this self-protective response.

CHAPTER 3

THE FIGHT/FLIGHT/FREEZE RESPONSE
The Heart of Repetitive Sports Performance Problems

To understand what happens to athletes struggling in the clutches of an RSPP, we turn to the animal kingdom. The predator-generated stress that prey animals experience in the wild illustrates the heart of STSD and its baffling symptoms. We believe that all RSPPs are a function of our built-in survival mechanism, the *fight/flight/freeze* response, gone awry. In fact, ***most RSPPs are a direct result of the athlete repeatedly getting stuck in the final survival option, the freeze response***. The fine work of Peter Levine (*Waking the Tiger—Healing Trauma*) is instructive here.

According to Levine, animals in the wild have a built-in "orienting response" that helps them periodically scan the environment for signs of predators and impending danger. This orienting response is an animal's early warning system and is responsible for keeping the animal safe during its daily routine of feeding, socializing, and mating. When an animal picks up any indication of threat through its senses, it stays hypervigilant until convinced the danger either was a false alarm or has passed. Should the orienting response correctly determine a life threat present in the animal's environment, however, the animal's physiology instantly ramps up to prepare it to fight or flee. Heart rate increases, muscles tighten, and respiration becomes rapid and shallow to ready the animal to either confront the attacker or run for its life. Should either survival option prove effective and eliminate the danger, the animal's physiology gradually returns to normal and it resumes its previous activities.

Should the fight/flight attempts fail, however, leaving the animal about to be caught and devoured by the predator, the prey animal instinctively uses the final survival strategy: *freezing*. The trapped animal instantly falls to the ground in a frozen, lifeless state as all of its vital functions briefly plunge. This immobility occurs for three reasons. First, some predators don't like to eat dead prey which, the animal appears to be when in this frozen state; second, predators tend to be less attentive to prey they believe is dead, making escape more possible; and third, this physiologically altered freeze state protects the numbed animal from suffering should the predator kill and eat the animal.

Prey animals go into freeze

If the predator loses interest in its seemingly dead meal and wanders off, leaving the opportunity for the prey to emerge from its freeze state, the animal twitches and trembles its entire body as it literally shakes off the residual effects of the freeze response. Through this natural shaking process, the animal regains full control of its body and fully releases the terrifying experience. When this is completed, the animal returns to the wild and resumes its life *as if nothing has happened*. Shaking off the effects of its brush with death allows the animal to **completely** and **fully** discharge all of the energy that was mobilized for survival. This shaking release enables the animal to go on with its life free of lasting negative aftereffects, which in humans we call trauma symptoms.

Unlike our animal cousins, human beings have been blessed with more fully evolved brains. For better or worse, this has allowed us to think, analyze, and reason our way to a place of dominance atop the animal kingdom. As a species, we are no longer primarily preoccupied with day-to-day survival. Consequently, our orienting and survival instincts are not as necessary for our typical daily living. The thinking brain has helped us transcend the age-old "survival of the fittest" struggle; however, a major downside of this brain evolution is that it has compromised our ability to effectively move through our instinctive fight/flight/freeze response. What does this mean?

According to Peter Levine, our thinking brain often second-guesses our inherent ability to take life-saving action. When confronted with a life-threatening situation, the rational mind may get confused and override survival instincts. This can lead straight into freezing and immobilization. To complicate matters, our modern culture views the instinctive surrender of the freeze response as a sign of weakness or cowardice. It's this negative judgment of a *natural process* that leads us to unconsciously fight the freeze response. By so interrupting this natural discharge, we never fully release the energy that originally mobilized for fight or flight.

When we are competing in sports, we are reenacting the survival of the fittest in a safe environment. The victor and the vanquished still exist, but all is done in play; we live to compete another day. The physicality enhances the discharge that sports provides for us, which is why we are driven to do it, but this "safe" competition isn't entirely safe, as sports injuries are so prevalent, and some competitions are more aggressive than others. When the stakes are raised by audiences, coaches, parents, and the media, the sense of danger is brought closer to the surface. ***Our response to danger is hard-wired in our brains and bodies and these survival mechanisms are totally involuntary and instinctive, so we don't have conscious control over when our systems perceive a threat in real life or on the court or field.*** This is why we can *automatically* go into survival mode on the mound with bases loaded, standing over a six-foot putt on the 18th, getting ready to shoot crucial free throws, or going for a back handspring on balance beam. In sports we rely on our instincts, but our instincts can also get in our way.

The very best athletes in the world are attuned to their instinctual roots. In fact, great athletes like Roger Federer or Tiger Woods are frequently described as being "natural" and "instinctive"; they have a natural feel for their games and always seem to know what to do regardless of how much pressure they are under. In these demanding situations they have an uncanny ability to simply trust the wisdom of their bodies and allow their performances to *just flow*.

Athletes who struggle with RSPPs have stopped trusting their instincts and instead attempt to consciously "coach" themselves through the performance. The more pressure they're under, the more conscious instructions they feed themselves. This over-thinking totally disrupts automatic, effortless execution and is a hallmark of RSPPs. We see this in mental mistakes, blown plays, slumps, and the yips.

The movement away from our instinctual nature is reflected in the view that the shaking that moves us out of freeze response is a sign of weakness. This is especially true in the macho world of competitive sports, where the demand to be physically and mentally "tough" encourages athletes to ignore and override their bodies' natural instincts.

When athletes are hurt, they are expected to "walk it off," "suck it up," or simply "play through" the pain. Our sports culture of "toughness" directly and indirectly encourages athletes to ignore their injuries.

Sports injury/sports trauma

The athlete's willingness to do so is rewarded by his or her coaches and teammates with praise and respect and is seen as a sign of strength and character. The athlete who chooses instead to listen to the wisdom of his or her body and thus avoid the risk of further injury is often viewed with contempt.

We tend to respond negatively to someone who's physically shaking as a result of an athletic injury. Our socialized response is to interrupt this "sign of weakness" and tell the athlete to pull himself together. "Tough" athletes don't shake! The shaking and twitching are the body's reflexes releasing the pent-up energy initially mobilized to deal with the shock of trauma, however. By interrupting this instinctual release, we inadvertently interfere with the ability to move through and get beyond the athletic trauma, and this interrupts the fluid and precise movement required in all sports.

The more we move away from our instinctual nature, the more difficulty we will have constructively resolving physically and emotionally upsetting experiences. These unresolved traumas silently accumulate over time, making athletes vulnerable to RSPPs. Ignoring an injury, downplaying its severity, and trying to stoically play through the pain are ineffective coping strategies. They encourage the athlete to further distance herself from her brain and body's instinctive ability to physically and emotionally heal itself. Sports are all about bouncing back, and our resilience is what makes this rebounding possible.

Physical and emotional traumas are an inevitable part of life for the competitive athlete. Because these traumas lie at the very root of all RSPPs, it is imperative to understand the freeze response and its disruptive effect on athletic performance when the natural movement out of this immobility state is interrupted. We believe that this information is vital for not only the struggling athlete, but all athletes. Even high-functioning athletes are adapting around the remnants of sports injuries and sports traumas. A low handicap in golf or a .300 batting average in baseball or softball can be improved (we call this sports performance expansion) by clearing away this debris.

THE SYMPTOMS OF TRAUMA ON AND OFF THE PLAYING FIELD

Exposure to repeated traumatic experiences on or off the playing field eventually leads to some level of the symptoms of repetitive performance problems *if these physically and emotionally upsetting events aren't properly healed in the athlete's mind and body*. It's the more severe symptoms of trauma that sports psychologists, coaches, and athletes and

Triathlete, Angela Bancroft after bike crash

their parents are naturally preoccupied with when it comes to any performance problem, but all athletes have trauma symptoms to some degree even if they don't get noticed or labeled as such. Slumps that are too frequent or that last too long are a good example of this. The varied symptoms of trauma are covered in the paragraphs below.

ANXIETY—Athletes talk about a "fog of anxiety" that can envelop them during warmups or the game. A Division I soccer player described this "fog" following her onto the playing field and sometimes staying with her the entire game, blocking her from playing up to her level. A college back-stroker injured when he slammed into the swimming pool wall on a turn complained of a sense of overwhelming dread every time he approached the wall in a big race. A pro golfer with the yips described being plagued by paralyzing anxiety whenever he pulled his putter out of his bag on the green. Sometimes an athlete is able to clearly articulate exactly what she is anxious about. At other times the athlete is at a total loss to explain where the anxiety is coming from. Anxiety is a classic symptom of trauma and PTSD and will always be found in those athletes who struggle with repetitive performance problems.

ANTICIPATORY ANXIETY AND PANIC ATTACKS— Anticipatory anxiety is another classic symptom of athletes suffering from trauma and RSPPs. Anticipatory anxiety is an explicit *fear of the future*, an intense worry about specific events happening, usually negative events that have already occurred. For many athletes who struggle with RSPPs, anticipatory anxiety is often directed at either their performance difficulty continuing or fear of reinjury. As a practice or competition approaches, the athlete is plagued by the "what ifs" (What if I strike out again? What if I fall? What if I land on my neck? What if *IT* happens again?). Sometimes this anxiety can be so intense that the athlete becomes totally immobilized and slips into a freeze state. When anxiety reaches this level of intensity, the athlete often experiences a *panic attack*. During a panic attack, the individual is totally overwhelmed by fear, can't catch his breath, and may experience chest pains, heart palpitations, and/or dizziness. It's not unusual for panic attack sufferers to mistakenly believe they are having heart attacks. Former Mets catcher Mackey Sasser described being besieged by these kinds of anxiety attacks the night before games in which he'd have to start behind the plate. This anticipatory anxiety makes the athlete vulnerable to avoidance of the activity.

*AVOIDANCE BEHAVIOR—*Avoidance behavior often accompanies intense anxiety and is a natural aftereffect of any traumatic experience. The trauma sufferer tends to avoid the behaviors, environment, situations, or reminders of the upsetting experience. A goal keeper who is kicked in the head while attempting to stop a shot, not surprisingly, will be "gun shy" the next time he has to come out of the goal to contest a ball in the box. Similarly, the swimmer who had a frightening asthma attack in the middle of her mile will only want to race her shorter events. Sometimes the athlete is consciously aware of his avoidance, but at other times, the avoidance behavior is manifested unconsciously. For example, the athlete may mysteriously get sick or injured right before she has to face the source of this anxiety. Intense stomach pains, throwing up, incapacitating muscle cramps, or freak last-minute injuries make it "impossible" for the athlete to compete and thus save him from having to directly face the source of his fear.

DISSOCIATION—When an athlete suddenly can't get his or her body to do what it already knows how to do (throw a strike, execute a round-off back handspring back-tuck, make a simple chip shot, or throw the ball back to the pitcher, for example), he or she is experiencing a state of *dissociation. It's as if those long-used skills and the muscle memory involved in them have suddenly been physically and mentally locked away from the athlete's conscious access*. Dissociation always involves a splitting off or separation of thoughts and/or physical feelings from normal consciousness. Sometimes this dissociation is directly experienced as a feeling of *numbness* in an athlete's extremities as she literally loses her feel of the skills. At other times, the athlete just can't seem to get himself to go for or execute the skill, as if there is another, more unconscious part deliberately holding him back. Dissociation is characterized by either a partial or complete loss of memory and connection to self. Dissociation is also clearly visible in the freeze response when the athlete's body completely shuts down. Whether physical, mental, or emotional, dissociation is a hallmark symptom of most trauma sufferers and is always visible in the athlete struggling in the clutches of a repetitive performance problem.

STATE OF CONFUSION—Many athletes who suffer from trauma-driven RSPPs also talk about a *state of confusion* (which is related to anxiety and dissociation) that they just can't seem to shake. They sometimes complain about not being able to "think straight" or get their minds to work. They appear to be somewhat lost either before or during the performance. The gymnast who forgets where she is in the middle of her beam routine and the tennis player who continues to hit to his opponent's strength during the match both demonstrate this state of confusion.

HYPERAWARENESS OF PHYSICAL SENSATIONS— Trauma sufferers are *hyperaware of the physical sensations* that they feel in their bodies. It is as if the "volume control" of their internal experience is turned up too high and is stuck there. Sometimes this hyperawareness is directly linked to a previous injury or trauma. In these cases, the athlete is obsessively preoccupied with the vulnerability of this particular part of his body. For example, a high school basketball player tore the ACL of her right knee the previous season and now can't seem to get herself to stop obsessively searching for similar physical sensations in her knee whenever she practices or plays. At other times, this hyperawareness seems to focus on a physical feeling that is part of the performance problem. For example, a high school catcher suffering debilitating throwing problems couldn't stop himself from focusing on the tension in the thumb of his throwing hand. Whenever he couldn't accurately throw the ball back to the pitcher, this tension would always emerge. His hyperawareness generated even more anxiety, making a natural throw impossible.

NEGATIVE SELF-TALK AND DISTORTED SELF-BELIEFS—Another characteristic of trauma sufferers is being plagued by an overabundance of negative thinking.

This continual flow of negativity contributes to the distorted beliefs that they end up maintaining about themselves. The athlete attempting to free himself from the clutches of an RSPP is also flooded by negative self-talk ("I suck," "I'm a failure") whenever he prepares to perform. The negative self-talk erodes self-confidence, raises anxiety, and distracts the athlete's focus from what's important. A talented cross-country runner who inexplicably lost her energy midway through all of her races couldn't control her thinking that her competitors were better than her, even though her times proved otherwise. Similarly, a national-caliber figure skater was often overwhelmed by negative thinking and self-doubts right before she had to begin her long program.

PHYSICAL TENSION—Increased muscle tension is another common byproduct of struggling with the unresolved aftereffects of trauma. Sometimes this muscular tension is localized around the injury site, and at other times, it is experienced all over the body. Whether injury-related or not, excessive physical tension is most often generated by all of the aforementioned symptoms, especially anxiety. This physical tightness is the primitive, protective bracing or crouch that we instinctively adopt whenever we're confronted by physical danger. Because one of the primary secrets to peak performance is staying loose and relaxed both *before* and *during* performance, tight muscles always make smooth execution impossible. One can always find excessive muscle tension in athletes struggling with RSPPs. The ski racer who consistently had trouble finishing his races following a bad fall complained of excessive muscle tightness right before he got into the starting gate. The softball pitcher who had suddenly lost her control and confidence talked about not being able to loosen up in warmups or on the mound. **Playing sports while carrying muscle tension, even microscopically, makes one much more susceptible to injury, so a circle exists in which sports injuries lead to**

sports trauma and sports traumas then lead to sports injuries.

All of these physical and emotional symptoms (anxiety, avoidance behavior, dissociation, confusion, panic attacks, hyperawareness of physical sensations, negative self-talk and distorted beliefs, and physical tension) are the more conscious, visible byproducts of brushes with *trauma. We instinctively experience these events as life-threatening.* It may seem difficult to understand how an athlete could experience a simple act of throwing a baseball back to the pitcher or of trying to stop a shot on goal as a *life-threatening* event, but *internally, this is exactly what goes on for the athlete whose fight/flight/freeze response has been automatically triggered.* Because of the athlete's unique personal and injury histories, he perceives himself as being in danger. Although the memory of the underlying trauma(s) may be lost from the athlete's conscious awareness, she continues to respond as if the threat to life and limb is still present. The athlete's threat response to what appears to coaches, teammates, and spectators as a routine situation makes the performance problem all the more baffling.

"Deer in headlights" illustrates freeze response

It's important to keep in mind that the trauma symptoms that we've been discussing are not actually **caused** by the triggering event or the trauma itself. Instead, *they stem from the energy that has been trapped in the athlete's nervous system that has never had a chance to fully release.*

FIGHT/FLIGHT IN SPORTS—AN INCOMPLETE PICTURE

Traditional sports psychology has long recognized the symptoms, but not the causes, of the fight/flight survival instincts involved with repetitive performance problems. When most sport psychologists work with RSPPs, they primarily focus on the high level of anxiety within the athlete, the so-called "bad nervous." Their theory is that although some level of pregame excitement or arousal ("good nervous") is necessary for peak performance, too little or too much arousal right before the start will always lead to subpar performances. As a result, most sports psychologists tend to directly target this preperformance anxiety in an attempt to reduce it. Their goal is to help the athlete reach a state of optimal arousal, or "good nervous," (we believe "no nervous" is achievable and ideal) right before the start of the contest. They do this by teaching athletes first how to recognize where their anxiety is coming from and then how to systematically lower the anxiety by using specific relaxation techniques. As we've outlined here, however, the performance-disrupting anxiety within the athlete doesn't exist on its own; it is instead a surface symptom of deeper experiences. Though it is beneficial for an athlete to master relaxation techniques, these conscious techniques alone do not **consistently** reduce an athlete's preperformance anxiety level. Why?

This nervousness isn't always the fight/flight response being triggered. Frequently, it is a byproduct of the final stage of this survival reflex, the freeze response. When you're "frozen in fright," using conscious relaxation techniques to calm yourself is ineffective and at times deepens the freeze. Unless the freeze has been found and released, it will return again and again.

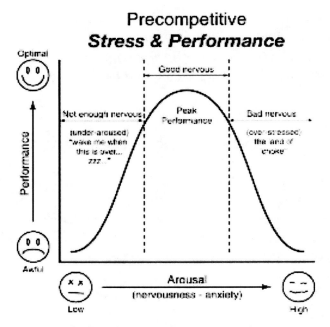

Traditional sports performance arousal curve

With all RSPPs, the athlete's survival instincts end up interfering with his or her performance. Humans' minds and bodies are wired together for survival. Fine-tuned athlete's minds and bodies are wired together for optimal performance. We've repeatedly observed that the performance-disrupting problems (choking, slumps, crippling fear, and the yips) in all sports come directly from the repeated triggering of false survival alarms within the athlete. The reflexes that athletes depend on get conditioned through many thousands of hours of skill training and repetitions in practice. ***When an athlete faces a situation similar to his original trauma or injury, his body is triggered into the fight/flight/freeze response and the developed skill reflexes quickly go offline.***

For example, a pitcher who has been hit in the head by a line drive back up the middle finds his survival reflexes triggered when he takes the mound. Pitching entails the forward momentum of the pitcher's arm, leg, and body ***toward*** the plate, the source of the athlete's past trauma. The pitcher's reflex of ***moving forward*** is countered by the powerful survival reflex of ***moving away*** to protect himself from another trauma.

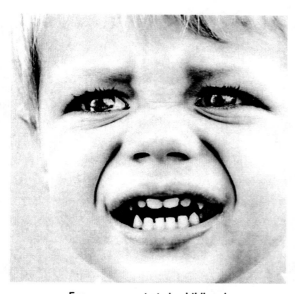

Fear response starts in childhood

This survival reflex can get automatically reactivated by any number of things in the athlete's immediate environment. Simply walking out to the mound while holding the ball or watching an imposing power hitter step into the box can be a trigger. Hearing the crack of the ball on the bat or seeing the ball heading straight back up the middle can reactivate the trauma for the athlete. For example, a Division I softball pitcher who had been struck by a line drive in the forehead reflexively ducked anytime a ball was hit back at her, regardless of the speed of the ball. This was especially frustrating for both her and her coach when she instinctively ducked under easily catchable soft line drives.

The athlete is totally unaware that this inner conflict is going on, fueling his performance difficulties. He may be on the mound and feeling vaguely uncomfortable, or he may be aware that he lacks his signature control, movement, or velocity. In 2005, Red Sox pitcher Matt Clement was hit in the head and knocked out by a line drive back up the middle. When Clement was finally cleared to return several weeks later, he was again struck hard, this time in the leg. From that point on, his earned-run average spiked along with his walk percentage as his control did a disappearing act. On the mound he was probably struggling back and forth between fight/flight panic and the freeze interruption of his fluidity. Soon after, Clement injured his pitching arm and was put on the disabled list. As mentioned earlier in this chapter, we see this frequently, as tightened muscles from the freeze response are more vulnerable to injury. It is unknown how many sports injuries stem from playing while tight, even "micro-tight," which certainly would be out of the athlete's awareness.

Think of a child who lets his hand wander too close to a hot stove. The child very quickly learns not to do this and reflexively pulls his hand back to avoid burning his hand again. In this case, the traumatic experience of the pain appropriately teaches the child ***never*** to put his hand on a hot stove. Unfortunately, the traumatized pitcher doesn't have a choice in the matter. Because it's his job, he must return to his "hot stove," the mound, time and time again with every start he makes and every pitch he throws. As he begins his windup and delivery, his forward momentum then triggers his survival response of pulling back. As a result, the pitcher might unconsciously pull his wrist or hand back, not shift his weight completely forward, or simply flinch as he throws. He may squeeze the ball, hold onto it too long, or let go of it too soon. Pitching well is a matter of inches, and these anomalies can throw it off by feet.

A talented ski racer who had suffered a bad fall the previous season could not get himself to stay low and forward during his races.

Skier able to stay low and in balance

Instead, he always found himself sitting back and up on his skis, significantly slowing his downhill times. Although his muscle memory and performance reflexes had been finely tuned to stay low, lean into his edges, and go as fast as possible, his survival reflexes were doing just the opposite, keeping him high and back on his skis so he would go slower and be safer. We commonly know such actions as fighting ourselves.

In the next chapter, we further illustrate how physical injuries unconsciously accumulate in an athlete's body and ultimately show themselves as a performance problem. In Calder's story, we will highlight how the body's instinctive, self-protective fight/flight/freeze response interfered with the optimal pitching performance of a talented college pitcher.

CHAPTER 4

CALDER'S STORY
Athletic Injuries, Performance Problems, and Perseverance

In this chapter we share with you the story of Calder, a college pitcher who suddenly and inexplicably developed control problems in his freshman year. His struggles on the mound became so acute that they threatened to derail his college career and his lifelong dream of playing professional ball. Calder's story illustrates the development of RSPPs, their relationship to sports injuries, and the role played by experiences encompassing an individual's life history. This chapter also reveals how the treatment process works not only in targeting the performance problem but in treating the athlete as a whole person. Calder's story is unique because it represents a long-term treatment situation spanning several years. This length of treatment was necessitated by an extensive injury history and the fact that Calder suffered repeated reinjury during the course of his work with me (DG).

What is especially powerful about Calder's story is the profound impact that this kind of therapy tends to have on the athlete in his or her life *outside of sports. We have found that to heal performance, we must also heal the person. This is because the psychological and physical wounds underlying every RSPP are in the person, not in the performance.* For example, it may seem like common sense to athletes, coaches, and parents that *performance anxiety* is simply a *performance problem* and is corrected by changing certain performance variables such as concentration, physiological arousal level and/or ability to handle negative self-talk. In our experience, this is incorrect. Significant

Calder Kaufmann on mound

performance anxiety does not exist without anxiety also being present in other aspects of a person's life; therefore, it is imperative that the psychological help that the athlete receives not only address his or her performance difficulty but, more importantly, directly deals with the person struggling with the problem. When an athlete gets the right kind of psychological help, profound changes are catalyzed within, leaving the athlete a happier, healthier person, not simply an athlete who is better able to perform.

Calder was initially referred to me (DG), during spring semester of his freshman year at Grand Valley State, a Division II college in western Michigan. Calder had entered Grand Valley the previous fall carrying the heavy burden of high expectations. As a talented, dedicated, hardworking athlete, the 6'6", 215-pound righty was a control pitcher with reasonable speed and good stuff. He had been the star of his high school team and believed that he could make a similar contribution at a collegiate level. His high school coach had not only shared Calder's beliefs but felt that his graduating senior had the stuff to make it to the majors. Calder's dad, who had been his son's pitching coach "since birth," shared this belief. Calder had been heavily recruited by Grand Valley State, given a partial scholarship, and expected to make an impact in the starting rotation, a rarity for a "true freshman."

Calder threw well enough in fall ball of his freshman year, his fastball touching 90 mph for the first time; however, for the very first time in his pitching career, he found that his control was inconsistent. Initially, it wasn't anything more serious than occasionally missing his spots. As these misses began to increase, however, Calder began experiencing increasing anxiety both before and during practice. This anxiety was exacerbated by his high expectations, the pressure from coaches, and the awareness that he was playing ball at a much higher level. Being separated from his family for the first time in his life intensified his stress.

Anxiety wasn't new to Calder, as he had grown up with an underlying anxiety disorder. He had suffered from asthma as a child, and his anxiety was fueled by his difficulty in breathing. Asthma had landed him in the local emergency room on several occasions and instilled a fear of hospitals. At age 15, he'd had his first panic attack but had been able to cope with it and subsequent ones while still living at home.

Calder's reaction to his mysterious control problem was classic: obsessing about it on and off the field, worrying if it would progressively worsen each time he threw. As his throwing woes continued, he responded like most athletes do to a RSPP: He "tried harder" to fix the

Calder in high school

problem. He spent more time practicing on his own, sometimes to the point that his arm ached. When he was on the mound, he began to "aim" the ball, attempting to better control the locations of his pitches. Predictably, the more he thought about location and the harder he tried to consciously direct his pitches, the tighter he got physically and the less control he had. As these failed attempts mounted, he became increasingly consumed with his throwing, "thinking about it 24/7." Calder's throwing difficulties seemed to be physically centered in his right hand, where he experienced a tightness that radiated up into his forearm.

As fall ball progressed toward the final, three-game, intra-squad "World Series" to be played in front of family and friends, Calder threw quite well, but this was the calm before the storm. –Five to six hours before every start, he battled increasing waves of anxiety. He worried about what his teammates and coaches would think of him. He felt guilty that he had been recruited for his talent and now couldn't deliver. *He was plagued by the* "what ifs" that relentlessly raced through his head. "What if I can't find the strike zone? What if I hit more batters? What if I have a panic attack on the mound?" These worries generated so much fear that Calder contemplated ways to avoid having to pitch that day. For the very first time in his life, the joy and anticipation that had always been part of an approaching game had been replaced by dread.

On the mound, Calder tried to turn things around by using positive self-talk to force his body to override the growing doubt, anxiety, and physical tension. He continuously reminded himself that he'd done this successfully countless times over the years, dominating hitters in the process. He told himself that he was untouchable and coached himself to "slow down," "relax," and "breathe." He tried to barricade himself behind a wall of positive thinking and self-confidence, but no matter what he told himself, the wall crumbled around him. His positive thoughts proved no match for the doubts and anxiety that threatened to overwhelm him at any moment.

Calder had first experienced anxiety symptoms on the mound during a playoff game as a high school senior. Anxiety had never infiltrated his baseball world before then, but Calder's nervousness lasted only an inning or two and didn't negatively affect his throwing. As his pitches got wilder that freshman fall, however, the "devil" in his head reminded him of this high school incident, predicting that it might happen again in college.

Calder made it through the end-of-season "World Series" without major incident and actually threw quite well in the third and final game, picking up the win. Despite the fact that he had thrown acceptably on the outside, however, all was not well on the inside. He couldn't shake the feeling that something was very wrong with him and that somehow he was still going to lose control again. The more he worried, the tighter his throwing hand and arm became.

In early January, a week after Calder returned to school after Christmas break, things seemed to go from bad to worse. He and his teammates helped the coaching staff run a baseball camp for mid-teens. Calder was behind the plate, catching a 15-year-old who was receiving instruction from Grand Valley's head coach. When Calder threw the kid's first pitch back, the ball inexplicably sailed five feet *over* the youngster's outstretched glove. Calder was dumbfounded. It felt as if someone had taken control of his arm, deliberately interfering with his throwing motion. He was left in a state of shock and humiliation. His worst nightmare was finally happening.

After catching the kid's second pitch, Calder again had that same loss-of-control feeling as he released the ball. This time he bounced his return throw into the dirt, well in front of the young pitcher. Calder was swept under by a wave of anxiety that clouded his thinking, blurred his vision, and choked his breathing. He felt like he was in a fishbowl with everyone in the gym witnessing his humiliating failure. When his third throw sailed high over the pitcher's head, the floodgates of anxiety opened. Calder's heart began racing; he became dizzy and "foggy" and was certain that unless he escaped the gym immediately, he was going to pass out.

For the very first time in his life, he couldn't throw a baseball, and it shook him to the core. He made some excuse to the coach about not feeling well and then hurriedly exited the gym, awash in shame and anxiety. It didn't help that his best friend came up to him later and half-demanded, "What the hell was going on with you out there? You know how embarrassing that was for everyone?" Calder spent the rest of the day in a fog, consumed by what had just happened and plagued by the question, How can I possibly get the ball over the plate when I can't even throw it back to the pitcher?" His worries about missing his spots had morphed into the concern that he wouldn't be able to accurately pitch the ball to the catcher. Suddenly, he was embarrassed to be around his teammates and began to dread throwing in their presence.

A few days later, Calder's baffling nightmare continued. While warming up indoors, throwing to his coach with a batter at the plate, he couldn't hit the coach's mitt. He either bounced the ball or threw it over the batter's head. Later that same day, Calder had to throw to live batters in the cage. Miraculously, he had managed to calm himself and seemed to warm up just fine; however, the thought that he'd now have to pitch to big, seasoned hitters reactivated his anxiety. Of the 50 pitches that he threw, only two or three crossed the plate, the rest far outside the strike zone. In the process, Calder hit a number of his teammates, which greatly affected him. Not only was he not giving his teammates good pitches to work on their swings, but he was "bouncing fastballs off them like it was going out of style."

His anxiety spiked from this surreal experience, and again he had that dizzy, foggy feeling. It was as if he was outside his body witnessing the horror and shock. Pitching had been a constant in his life, the anchor that he could count on for stability, confidence, and identity. Now, inexplicably, it was gone.

Calder delivering

By February, Calder's pitching had regressed to the point that he couldn't throw the ball 15 feet. A month later, his coaches red-shirted him for the duration of the season. Though their decision proved to be a tremendous relief to him, Calder hated himself for having this reaction. As the season progressed, he avoided throwing with the team, claiming that his arm was sore. Instead, he went off by himself late at night and threw a tennis ball against a wall until his arm hurt; however, this trusted coping strategy of "trying harder" felt more like "bashing my head against a wall."

Calder's throwing problem was completely baffling to him, his coaches, and his family. How could an experienced pitcher with so much talent, speed, and control be reduced to someone who couldn't accurately throw a baseball 15 feet?

The answer to Calder's mystery can be found in the nature of sports. Sports is like a pinball machine; it's all about *movement.* It's impossible to be a *moving* athlete without eventually colliding with another moving athlete or an immovable object. Falling, frightening close calls, and injury are a normal and sometimes painful part of the moving sports experience. Every athletic career is littered with numerous physical and emotional traumas. Starting from when the athlete begins to run, throw a ball, or swing a bat, club, or racquet, and continuing through his or her entire sports career, the athlete is vulnerable to suffering these athletic upsets. Of course, the injuries aren't simply confined to the field, track, or court. Athletes also get injured outside of sports in their daily lives, but the likelihood of sustaining an injury is increased by the movement of playing sports.

As we've been discussing throughout this book, *the physical and psychological injuries sustained by an athlete unconsciously accumulate over time in the body until they reach a critical mass.* This was the clearly the case with Calder. His inexplicable control problem, like all RSPPs, had a trauma/injury base.

Physically and emotionally upsetting experiences do not naturally process through like other life events. They are frozen in their entirety within the athlete's brain-body system. These unprocessed experiences with their visual, emotional, physical, and mental components form the invisible seeds of the later emergence of repetitive performance difficulties.

Sports injury/sports trauma

When and how this happens depends on a variety of factors including the athlete's personal and trauma history, genetic blueprint, personal strengths and vulnerabilities, underlying psychological issues like depression or anxiety, and relationships with parents, siblings, and coaches.

Eventually, the athlete experiences a pivotal event that triggers the emergence of the images, anxiety, physical tension, and self- doubt. The trigger can be another injury, an upsetting experience with a coach or parent, or, as in Calder's case, just simply ***having to perform under an increased level of pressure***. Suddenly, the athlete finds herself struggling with excessive performance anxiety or diminished self-confidence. Perhaps for the very first time in her sports history, the athlete can't seem to get the job done. She seems unable to control her body and has difficulty executing basic and simple athletic tasks, movements that used to be flawless and without thought.

This is Calder's story. The final straw was the intense pressure from having to perform at the higher level of college ball. The expectation that he excel on this bigger stage touched off problems that had long been brewing just below his awareness. Events from his personal and injury history were ultimately responsible for laying the foundation for this later emergence of his repetitive throwing difficulties.

As a five-year-old, Calder suffered from severe asthma that repeatedly landed him in the emergency room. These attacks were accompanied by anxiety that left him feeling trapped and contributed to his fear of hospitals. This fear remained with him until a year before he graduated college and was released during our treatment.

Calder's first injury resulted from overuse and occurred during little league. He simultaneously pitched for three teams and developed *a severe tendonitis in his throwing elbow*. Although Calder recovered quickly, this kind of trauma left his arm vulnerable to future problems.

Calder's grandmother lived with his family when he was 15. He'd had a close, loving relationship with her his entire life. She moved in suffering from congestive heart failure and poliomyelitis The poliomyelitis precipitated her death a few months after she moved, just before the start of Calder's sophomore year. This was a major loss for Calder because his grandmother had always been an important part of his life. It was in conjunction with her illness and death that he had his first anxiety attack. Halfway through the fall of that year, he became the starting quarterback for the JV team. The anxiety from losing his grandmother affected his ability to pass under pressure, fueling what he called "major anxiety attacks" during games. The connection between Calder's inability to handle the pressure of being the quarterback and his later pitching problems were uncovered later in our work.

As a senior, Calder became a starting wide receiver for varsity. In a big game, he leaped to reel in a pass and at the apex of his jump was popped by the defender. The force of the blow spun him around and caused him to land squarely on his throwing shoulder. He also sustained a severe concussion from the impact. The doctor who examined him thought nothing was structurally wrong with his shoulder and prescribed a brief course of physical therapy.

Early in the next spring, while playing first base, Calder ran into a fence while chasing a foul ball. The collision broke the middle finger of his throwing hand. *Because of medical incompetence, the injury went undetected for more than a year*. Consequently, his finger was

Calder(33) injures his throwing shoulder while tackling

constantly swollen, making it impossible for him to properly grip the ball. *Calder pitched both his senior year in high school and freshman year in college with this undiagnosed injury.*

In April of his freshman year at Grand Valley State, Calder hit an emotional low. His father decided to look for someone who might be able to help his son with his throwing problems. Calder's dad found my website while researching the yips and immediately set up an appointment. By this point, Calder was feeling hopeless. Nothing he had tried had helped him get a handle on his problem; instead, things had progressively worsened. He was skeptical of psychologists and didn't see how talking to someone on the phone could help him resolve a pitching problem. Calder's anxiety felt out of control, and the last thing he wanted was to talk with a total stranger about it.

Calder was caught in a spiral of anxiety, so my first goal was to help calm him. I took an extensive sports injury and personal history. At our first session, the death of his grandmother appeared to be a major trauma silently fueling his anxiety.

We also focused on the current source of his anxiety, the loss of control. We did this by addressing the two traumatic throwing experiences: first his humiliating loss of control as practice catcher in early January, and second, his subsequent wild practice outing against his Grand Valley State teammates.

Because trauma gets stuck in an athlete's brain and body, my aim was to help Calder process through these upsetting experiences and diminish his anxiety. In the early stages of this work, it's not unusual for things to worsen before they improve. The processing often resurfaces forgotten traumas, which temporarily increases the activation. This was the case in Calder's situation. When we first worked on the two trigger incidents, his anxiety and lack of confidence initially spiked; however, as we processed through some of his earlier injuries and anxieties, things began to shift positively and his distress level diminished.

As with most of the athletes who consult us, the work with Calder involved focusing on each trauma, dealing with present-day issues and anticipating future anxiety-provoking situations. A good deal of emphasis is placed on the athlete's physiological experience during the processing. What the traumatic experience feels like and where the

Masters level player, John Ziegler serving

athlete feels the trauma in the body in the moment are critical to our work. Why? ***Because the physical injuries that unconsciously fuel the yips, anxiety, and blocks are usually revealed by the athlete's body during the processing***. This process of getting out of the head and tuning into the body took Calder time to grasp. As he described it, "Being able to tune down the voice in my head and recognize subtle cues in my body is an art form."

One example of our focus on the body is micro-movement. Calder was guided to reenact his throwing motion in extreme slow motion. At times, we ask an athlete to reexperience an injury in this way, physically recreating the movements just before, during, and after impact. As an athlete does this, he or she begins noticing reflexive twitches, freezes, and areas of tension throughout the body. As Calder noticed any of these, he was to immediately hold the position, focus on the sensations, and observe the internal processing that ensued. Behind many of these reflexive twitches and freezes lie other forgotten sports traumas. By releasing these traumas, the micro-movement becomes increasingly smooth. The aim of this exercise is to deeply release the multiplicity of blocks held silently in the body.

The work progressed, and Calder returned home for the summer. His anxiety had lessened, but things had gotten only marginally better. Away from his Grand Valley State coaches and teammates, he was able to relax, and his throwing gradually improved. He was again able to pitch off the mound but was a shadow of himself, which devastated him. He signed up for summer ball, and his pitching was barely passable. He lost 10 mph on his fastball, with poor control, walking many batters and hitting some. The ball felt strange in his hand, and he reflexively gripped it more tightly. This death grip wreaked havoc with his release point, causing him to wildly throw high or bury the ball in the dirt. For as long as Calder could remember, the baseball had felt like a part of his hand, and its sudden alien feeling became a pervasive source of worry.

In late July, Calder had surgery to repair the broken finger on his throwing hand. It is important to note again that all surgeries are experienced as physical and emotional traumas to the brain and body and are stored that way. Accordingly, these effects need to be processed through like any other injury. We again used micro-movements while anticipating the trauma of the surgery and later to process through its aftereffects. By August, before he returned for the start of his sophomore year, Calder's hand was 100% healed.

When he returned to Grand Valley State for fall ball, Calder and his red-shirted teammates had to try out again for the team. In preparation, we focused on his anticipatory anxiety. Although Calder was able to function during the 10-day tryouts, he pitched poorly and was cut from the squad, along with all but one of the other red shirts. As in many high school and college programs around the country, the cutting process was callous and impersonal. No one took the time to sit down with Calder and explain the program's decision. It didn't matter that Calder had been recruited on the recommendation of a San Diego Padres scout or that his ability was head and shoulders above the other freshmen. This rejection was another powerful emotional trauma and left him feeling devastated and devalued.

Despite the emotional pain and frustration, Calder never considered quitting baseball. This is despite the fact that through this entire time, Calder was unknowingly pitching with an injured shoulder tracing back to high school football!

When someone sustains an injury to any part of the body, a natural protective reflex is triggered around the injury site to keep that part of the body safe. In Calder's case, pressure on his right shoulder triggered an impulse to "wing it," or hold his right elbow close to his body. *This self-protective response operates out of the athlete's consciousness and wreaks havoc on mechanics and control.* "Being on the edge of not being able to throw at all," Calder unconsciously responded to his shoulder's sense memory of the collision. His throwing shoulder was telling him self-protectively, "It's dangerous to throw the ball."

After getting cut from Grand Valley State's team, Calder immediately began looking for other teams where he could play. Shortly thereafter, he transferred to Grand Rapids Community College (GRCC), which boasted one of the best junior college baseball programs in the country. He started at GRCC in the spring of his sophomore year, and though his control problems and anxiety weren't as bad as in the previous year, they were both still active. Calder forced himself to go to practice and continued to work hard on his own in a desperate attempt to turn things around. The situation deteriorated for him right before the team's spring trip to Florida.

Calder was throwing indoors in a batting cage, pitching to his new teammates, when his anxiety suddenly spiked. As his nervousness rose, he felt claustrophobic, back in the fishbowl of exposure. As he got more anxious, his scant control over the ball was evaporated and he began hitting batters. The GRCC head coach, who was harsh and old-school, screamed at Calder in front of the entire team, "Hey K, get the f... out of the cage. Either you're a huge pussy or you're injured!"

Calder exited feeling humiliated and headed to the trainer to ice his arm. The experience plunged him to an all-time low, overwhelmed with hopelessness and depression. After discussing the situation with his parents, he decided to have his arm medically checked out.

Calder was seen by a surgeon who thought he might have a separated shoulder. Calder then sought out a second opinion with a shoulder specialist, the renowned Dr. James Andrews in Alabama. Andrews diagnosed the problem as a torn labrum and recommended immediate surgery, but Calder was unable to get his insurance to cover the cost on such short notice. Instead, he returned home and had his shoulder reexamined by the original doctor who had seen him after his football injury. A month later, the doctor performed arthroscopic surgery and discovered that the labrum was indeed badly torn. Calder was shocked to discover the seriousness of his injury, as he had long assumed that his throwing problems were solely psychological. We continued to process these traumatic incidents, including the meltdown in front of the GRCC coach, the shoulder injury, and the trauma of the surgery.

By mid-October, Calder had recovered enough to resume throwing, but it was too soon for a comeback from a major shoulder surgery. As a consequence, his right shoulder was stressed by his throwing and he unknowingly tore his labrum again. In retrospect, this second tear was far worse than the first, and Calder experienced it as weakness rather than pain. As a result of this injury, his shoulder began to sublux (pop out of the socket) whenever he threw at full speed. This happened with regularity, sometimes two to three times a pitching session, 30 to 40 times over the course of the season. His shoulder wasn't dislocated, however, and would automatically pop back into the socket.

Calder went back to GRCC for spring ball not knowing that he still had a torn labrum, and because the weakness in his shoulder wasn't debilitating, he was able to function well enough to blend in. While he still worried that he might lose control, his ongoing work with me helped him stabilize his anxiety to a manageable level. Even with his shoulder injured, he was able to pitch with control and without panic. As the season progressed, and his shoulder continued to pop out and in, however, his weakness while throwing increased and he started to feel increasing pain. Realizing something was wrong, Calder returned to the doctor who had performed his first shoulder surgery. This time, the surgeon decided to do an open procedure to tighten up Calder's shoulder capsule. When the surgeon opened up Calder's shoulder, he discovered that the labrum was badly torn.

The baseball can be a danger to both pitcher and batter

Through the following summer and after rehab, Calder was "95% back." He was once again able to pitch with control and without anxiety. He felt like he had been "reborn into baseball" and had shed the nagging dread in the back of his mind. We had effectively processed through his old traumas as well as the current ones from this tumultuous year. He was feeling good about himself and had enrolled in Aquinas College, an NAIA school, for his next-to-last year of athletic eligibility.

Calder made it through fall ball at Aquinas College without injury or performance problems, but before Christmas break, during a bullpen session, Calder was startled by tearing sounds coming from his shoulder. "It sounded like a tree branch being ripped from its trunk," he said. As he continued to throw, his shoulder suddenly popped out of the socket and stayed out. It was the most pain he had ever experienced. A little while later, the shoulder slipped back in, causing Calder even more discomfort. He went back to his surgeon, who suggested that he change his throwing motion from overhand to side-arm. For two weeks, Calder followed his doctor's advice and had five or six painful dislocations.

Remarkably, even as Calder's shoulder continued to dislocate, he experienced no control problems. Physically, his shoulder was far worse than ever, but mentally, he was calm and focused. At this point, he decided to get a second opinion and went out of state to consult with a top shoulder specialist. Dr. Craig Morgan practiced in the Maryland–Delaware area and was surgeon to a number of elite and professional athletes. Morgan had pioneered arthroscopic procedures for the shoulder and had written the protocols that most shoulder surgeons followed. When he arthroscopically examined Calder's shoulder, he discovered that the two previous surgeries had been badly botched.

Dr. Morgan operated on Calder's shoulder, Calder's third surgery in as many years. Calder spent the next three months in intensive rehabilitation. Although it would take him 18 months for a full recovery, by midsummer after this latest surgical intervention Calder was throwing over the top again, free from anxiety and with full control. He continued to work on strengthening the muscles in his shoulder. With this surgery, as with all the others, our work aimed to help Calder process through any residual physiological and emotional effects.

Calder continued to strengthen his shoulder over the fall and appeared to be finally heading in the right direction. By Christmas, his speed had climbed back to the low 80s and his control was "phenomenal."

It looked like he was again on track for being productive in college and having a shot at being drafted by the pros. Over the past three years, he had been to hell and back, both physically and emotionally. His struggles had taken him so far from his dreams that he often questioned whether he'd ever find his way back. In the process, he had endured unbearable humiliation, three surgeries, and rehab. As a consequence of our work, he felt like a "wiser, happier, more emotionally and socially competent me."

In February of the next year, however, he again began to experience weakness in his throwing arm, for the first time in months. He also noticed that his shoulder was making grinding and popping sounds. In response, Calder limited the amount of time he threw hard. During one of these 10-minute throwing sessions, his right shoulder painfully popped out of the socket in the exact same spot as before. Calder knew at that moment that his baseball dream was over. He saw a local physician, who assessed that although the shoulder joint was still in place, the ligaments in his shoulder had either loosened or once again torn.

Calder was confronted with a painful realization, one he had known he might have to face all along. If he continued to pitch, he would be at risk of suffering irreparable damage to his shoulder, which might impede his normal, everyday functioning. He made the sensible decision and retired as a player, choosing to stay with the team through the spring season to help out instead.

Despite the lack of a happily-ever-after baseball ending, Calder's experience with his throwing yips was ultimately life changing. "It was actually the best thing that could've happened to me because it forced me to directly face my anxieties. If baseball wasn't so important to me, I might never have dealt with all of this." Calder was significantly changed as a person, feeling calmer, happier, and far more balanced after his experiences. He completed his undergraduate degree and has now completed a master's degree in psychology. His plan is to work with athletes and help them overcome the same kinds of performance struggles that he has experienced.

Calder's story is a classic example of the importance of the athlete's physical and emotional health in effectively resolving RSPPs. In the next chapter, we will examine the important but often overlooked concept of the athlete as a person. All too often, coaches, fans, and even parents get overly focused on the outcome of the athlete's performances and specific performance problems. When this happens, the athlete as a unique, feeling individual gets lost. The end result of this depersonalization is that the athlete suffers even more emotional harm and the repetitive performance problems continue and worsen. The progressively downward spiral of most RSPPs can't be helped until those directly interacting with the athlete put the athlete's emotional well-being first.

CHAPTER 5

REPETITIVE SPORTS PERFORMANCE PROBLEMS AND THE ATHLETE AS A PERSON
I AM NOT JUST MY ATHLETIC PERFORMANCE

A distinguishing feature of great coaches is that they develop strong, *healthy* relationships with their athletes. It is clear that these coaches *genuinely care* about the well-being of their players beyond their performance. This includes all other aspects of the athletes' lives outside of the arena. For example, these coaches aren't interested in academics solely as it relates to athletic eligibility; they sincerely care about how their athletes perform in school because they understand the value of a good education. These coaches want their athletes to succeed in life when their athletic careers are over. In sum, they care about how their athletes feel as people and want the best for them.

Coaches of this stripe *view their players as people first* and *athletes second*. They understand that their players have feelings, needs, and dreams that intersect and sometimes conflict with their athletics. They know the value of establishing trust with their athletes and so act in a trustworthy manner. They also understand the importance of establishing a safe environment for their athletes where the athletes feel comfortable learning and taking risks. These coaches intuitively know that with safety, their athletes can truly relax, focus, and perform optimally.

Top coaches view their job more expansively than many of their colleagues. They see their role as *teaching important life skills and producing healthy, well-adjusted, individuals, not just training athletes to excel and win.*

Coaches can be supportive

Many coaches pay lip service to the importance of preparing young people to make contributions to society, yet few are emotionally developed and balanced enough to "walk the talk" and adopt this crucial role. The caring professionals genuinely have sports in perspective and understand that sports is a metaphor for life, rather than life itself.

Unfortunately, too many coaches have lost this perspective and act as if the game's outcome is the only thing that matters. They are emotionally insensitive individuals who place their own needs in front of their athletes' needs. Winning is the way that these coaches measure themselves and their athletes. Their preoccupation with outcome is fueled by an underlying fear of not measuring up and consequently losing their jobs or the possibility of advancement. This kind of fear can usually be traced back to a coach's own personal experiences as an athlete, including his or her trauma history.

Most insensitive coaches unknowingly follow specific patterns in their teaching, treating their athletes in a harsh manner similar to one that they were treated in decades earlier. This tough style is reflective of a military mentality and represents a great deal of what is problematic in coaching today. A big game is likened to a **battle** where winning and losing are equated with life and death. Athletes are treated like soldiers who must be **tough, brave, and hardened** to **survive.** In addition, these **soldiers** must be willing to sacrifice themselves and their bodies for the good of the team and the **success of the mission.**

Fortunately, athletic competition is **not live combat** and athletes are **not armed warriors** required to blindly follow a superior's orders. In battle, a soldier's feelings and sensitivities are totally irrelevant and potentially a deadly distraction to the immediate task at hand. In sports, however, an athlete's feelings and sensitivities are important and relevant to both the individual's and team's performance. Ignoring this by turning a competitive game into a life-and-death struggle is an unfortunate and damaging mistake.

Coaches can be destructive

To the insensitive coach, problems in the locker room or off the playing field are annoying distractions from the mission of winning. Athlete academic difficulties interest this kind of coach only as they directly threaten the success of the team. In this way, the insensitive coach overtly uses athletes to further his or her own reputation.

Playing for this kind of coach is a dehumanizing experience because the athlete isn't seen as an individual with feelings, needs, and sensitivities. As a result, the athlete is at risk of emotional and physical trauma. The insensitive coach is more likely to respond to an athlete's injury with suspicion and callousness rather than interest and empathy. He or she believes that the injured athlete *is being a baby* or *making a mountain out of a molehill* or *dogging it.* As a result, the coach will pressure the athlete to be *a good soldier, suck it up,* and *play through pain.* This attitude puts the athlete at risk of further, more serious injury and trauma, which ultimately emerge as RSPPs.

In 1995, *San Francisco Chronicle* sports columnist Joan Ryan wrote a scathing exposé about the physical and emotional abuse in the training of elite gymnasts and skaters. In *Little Girls in Pretty Boxes,* Ryan described how a gold medal-producing gymnastics coach and his wife ran what was referred to as "the Factory" in their Texas gym. They took promising young gymnasts from around the US and systematically weeded out the *weak, rebellious,* and *unappealing* to assemble a core of potential Olympians. They subjected these young girls to emotional and physical abuse under the guise of high-level coaching. They demanded complete subservience and closely monitored the girls' caloric intake to the point of starvation. They used coercion to "encourage" the girls to train and compete when injured and made use of both humiliation and intimidation as "coaching" tools.

In 2008, Jennifer Sey, the 1986 National Champion and one of the *products* of the Factory, wrote an exposé on the emotional and physical abuse that she and her teammates endured in their training. In *Chalked Up,* Sey chastised the extreme measures practiced by Bella and Marta Karoli as cruel and unnecessary to produce champions.

Although abusive coaches may temporarily show outward success, their depersonalizing coaching methods take a heavy toll. For every gymnast who becomes a Mary Lou Retton, countless others are discarded along the way with broken bodies and damaged psyches. Some end up with severe eating disorders, and others are so depressed and beaten down that they've attempted suicide. Many are left with debilitating physical problems from the chronic injuries and stunted growth

Lauren Cartmell doing dismount off of balance beam

they've suffered resulting from long periods of overwork and malnutrition.

Athletes who achieve success under emotionally punishing circumstances do so only in a *time-limited* manner. They may get to the top but tend to not stay there. The fear and loss of humanity can only fuel them so long before they collapse under the cumulative pressure. So much societal importance is placed on winning that the public and even some parents turn a blind eye to abuse by coaches in the pursuit of *success*.

A number of prominent college coaches are known for turning around programs and obtaining surprising results in the won-loss column within a few months. With their abrasive styles and mistreatment of their players, these coaches tend to quickly wear out their welcome and then move on. They leave behind the psychological and physical wreckage as a result of their inhumane approach.

The athlete who suffers an RSPP is more vulnerable with these kinds of coaches. Intense fear is a normal part of competitive gymnastics and, consequently, we see many athletes who can't get themselves to go for certain skills. Insensitive coaches have little tolerance for gymnasts who battle fears and blocks. These "head cases" are forced to go against their instincts, to throw the feared skill anyway, or are *kicked out* of the gym.

RSPPs quickly exhaust the unrelated coach's already limited supply of patience and teaching creativity. The coach pressures the athlete to get over the problem, and when this doesn't happen, quickly turns on the athlete. The coach will then either bench or make an example of the athlete, humiliating the athlete in front of teammates as a "motivational" tactic. These coaches are oblivious to the negative impact that their words and actions have on their athletes. This abusive behavior is experienced by the struggling athlete as added trauma and *always* exacerbates the RSPP.

The insensitive coach isn't the only one who is overly focused on the athlete's performance difficulties at the expense of the athlete's feelings. Even well-meaning coaches, parents, and sports psychologists get excessively preoccupied with the performance problem and lose sight of what's in the athlete's best interests. This is understandable, given that everyone, including the athlete, is mobilized in a frantic attempt to resolve the RSPP as soon as possible. When the important adults in his or her life ignore his needs, the athlete is further traumatized. This *depersonalization* is common in today's sports world at all levels. When winning supersedes the well-being of the athlete as a person, the athlete always suffers.

This over-inflated importance of performance outcomes reflects one of the most serious sports problems we face, and it fuels the silent epidemic of RSPPs in today's athletes. Nowhere is this clearer than in professional sports, where media and fans use this narrow *outcome lens* to obsessively assess athletes. Accordingly, a pro athlete is only as good and valuable to the team as his or her *latest* performances, but when a pro makes big contribution to the team's victory, he or she is treated as a hero by an adoring public. Fans then view the athlete as strong, masterful, and magical. The public makes these attributions while knowing nothing about the athlete's background, character, or values. If *our athletes* perform well, we project countless positive traits onto these "heroes." When athletes struggle or slump, however, we attribute to them opposite qualities. Suddenly, these heroes are now weak, *lazy, or untalented*. Our imagination-fueled projections turn negative, and just as we built these athletes up, we cruelly tear them down. They're now *overrated, selfish, or head cases* who can't stand up to competitive pressure. The sports media and fans then *diagnose* what is wrong with their former heroes. We forget that these athletes are more like us than we imagine. They are actually thinking, feeling, sensitive human beings, not feeling-less performing automatons.

In the summer of 2006, New York Yankees fans and the local sports media turned on future Hall of Famer Alex Rodriguez, then the highest-paid player in the game. Through the 2006 season, A-Rod led the majors in home runs, RBIs, runs scored, and extra-base hits. During 2004, his first season playing for New York, he became the youngest player to reach 350 home runs. During that season, he hit .286 with 36 home runs, 106 RBIs, and 112 runs scored. Despite A-Rod's great season, however, the Yanks lost to their arch-rivals, the Boston Red Sox, in the American League Championship Series, missing by one out, sweeping them to advance to the World Series.

In 2005, Rodriguez hit .321 and led the American League with 124 runs, 48 home runs, and 130 RBIs. He won the AL home run title, made the All-Star team, and was named the AL MVP; however, in the divisional playoffs against the Los Angeles Angels, A-Rod hit only .133 without driving in a run as the Yanks lost. During the 2006 season, A-Rod continued to put up Hall of Fame numbers, but a hitting slump followed by a string of uncharacteristic errors (clearly RSPPs) seemed to further turn the fans against him. In the divisional playoffs, A-Rod went 1 for 14 as the Yanks lost four straight to the Detroit Tigers. The fans and sports media were predictably merciless in their response, ripping A-Rod for "not caring" about the team, being ***spoiled and overpaid,*** and lacking the ability to come through when it counted the most. These accusations were made in the face of stats that prove Rodriguez to be one of the best all-around ball players of his era.

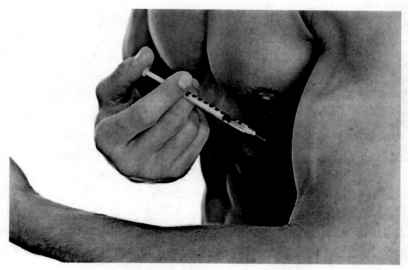

**Intense pressure has led some athletes
to abuse steroids**

What's interesting about this story is the latest chapter. It was brought to light in spring of 2009 that A-Rod had been using steroids and other performance-enhancing drugs. Although he said that his use was confined to a brief period when he played for the Texas Rangers, additional evidence has surfaced that points to his steroid use as far back as high school. The whole steroid issue points to the excessive amount of pressure these athletes are under to produce and the overemphasis on performance outcomes. This leads vulnerable athletes to pursue every edge, even when it is illegal or dangerous to their health.

In sports, just as in life, one can't adequately define someone simply by his or her performance of the moment. An athlete can't be accurately assessed by the narrow dimension of current performances on the field. Athletes are **human beings**, not one-dimensional creatures defined only by their latest results. Unfortunately, that is exactly how many coaches, parents, and sports fans view them. Good performances define athletes as good people, and bad performances characterize them as flawed.

Child athletes are easily traumatized

A game-winning hit or game-costing mistake doesn't capture the essence of the athlete as a performer or a person, but when parents and coaches define a child athlete by the quality of his performance, ignoring the child's feelings and needs, they abuse the child athlete, making him more vulnerable to suffering from psychological problems, especially RSPPs. We call this treatment of young athletes abusive because ignoring a child athlete's feelings and subjugating them to the feelings of adults is emotionally traumatic.

This one-dimensional view of athletes as performers is frequently, yet inadvertently, adopted by many sports psychologists who work with RSPPs. This occurs because the athlete and her coaches and parents involve the sports psychologist for one primary purpose: to *fix* the performance problem. The urgency to quickly get the job done can get in the psychologist's way, blinding him or her to what's going on for the athlete as a person. Because the commonly practiced model of sports psychology focuses on the athlete as a performer, what's most important gets lost. Accordingly, crucial information regarding the roots of the RSPP, and important clues about how to resolve it, are also missed.

Traditional sports psychology uses a cognitive-behavioral approach to help the struggling athlete conquer his performance problems. In this model, the athlete's difficulties are seen as resulting from unknowing use of *faulty mental strategies.* That is, the athlete's performance focus may be off, he may be too nervous right before the game, or he might be plagued by negative self-talk at crucial points during the performance. According to this cognitive-behavioral approach, these mistakes in thinking need to be corrected to restore the athlete's performance to an optimal level.

This process first entails helping the athlete increase awareness of how she is inadvertently contributing to the problem and then teaching her more adaptive mental strategies. Sports psychologists try to understand the specific faulty mental mechanics of the athlete and how they contribute to her RSPP. They then attempt to teach the athlete a set of mental skills that will eliminate the problem, replacing bad mental mechanics with good ones. This entire process is conducted on a *conscious* level because the RSPP is assumed to be ultimately under the athlete's control.   Because this process revolves around the athlete's *current* performances, important information from the athlete's history is left unexplored. *It is our absolute belief that this ignored information contains the secrets to both understanding and resolving RSPPs.*

There is no better example of this than former Mets catcher Mackey Sasser, who, as we saw in Chapter 1, suffered from the throwing yips, which prematurely ended his Major League career. Sasser was unable to throw the ball back to the pitcher without double and triple pumping it. Opposing runners successfully timed their delayed steals to Sasser's repetitive arm motion. It's notable that Sasser saw more than 50 professionals after his yips broke out, including psychiatrists, psychologists, sports psychologists, and hypnotists. *Not one* of these professionals ever asked Mackey about his injury history or personal trauma history; instead, they all focused directly on the superficial throwing problem and what might be done to eliminate it. As a result, none of these professionals were able to help Sasser.

In Mackey's case, as with all of the athletes we've worked with, the trauma and injury histories held the underlying causes of the problem along with the keys to its resolution. We have found that not taking the proper time to understand the athlete's performance difficulties *in the larger context* of his physical and emotional trauma history sets up frustration and failure. The roots of Mackey's yips stemmed from his traumas originating in his childhood and adolescence, not just the injuries that he sustained playing pro ball.

At times, an athlete's RSPP is a *direct* result of the pressures and expectations placed on him by coaches and parents. The athlete may be pushed to perform at a higher, more intense level than he aspires to himself. In these situations, the parents' or coaches' needs have outstripped the needs of the child athlete's. For example, one gymnast we worked with had inexplicably developed an incapacitating fear on the pommel horse on a skill he had been performing effortlessly for years. His mysterious fear made it impossible for him to compete in this event and created tremendous friction between the gymnast and his coaches.

When we looked at the gymnast's history, we discovered that he was physically and emotionally exhausted from three years of nonstop training and competition. He was no longer enjoying the sport and began questioning why he was doing it. His *block*, taken in the context of this *recent* history, was simply an unconscious attempt to create some psychological and physical space for himself. What he craved was time off and a chance to reassess what *he* really wanted out of *his* sport.

Simply examining an athlete's recent training and competition history doesn't provide enough information to *fully* understand the problem. The following case further illustrates the need to view the athlete and his or her performance problem in the larger context of his or her personal life.

Jeanne was a 50-year-old equestrian who resumed riding after a 33-year hiatus. Her presenting problem was an incapacitating fear of injury whenever she took a lesson or attempted to show in competition. When Jeanne went riding in the fields by herself, she was free of fear. She had returned to her sport after taking most of her adult life off. Her fear and performance difficulties emerged during her third year back, two months *after* she purchased her own horse. This was the first horse she had owned since she was 13. Shortly after her purchase, she began experiencing intense feelings of guilt in relation to the horse, an extremely good-natured animal.

A more traditional sports-psychology approach to Jeanne's problem would try to help her figure out how she was *scaring herself* right before lessons and competitions. The assumption would be that her fear was *self-generated* by her preperformance focus, thinking, and self-talk. If she gained awareness of these mental mistakes, she could then learn to correct them and thus calm herself. This approach would also guide Jeanne to observe how her concentration and self-talk were different when she rode solo. Developing an awareness of how she naturally employed these *adaptive* mental strategies would contribute to mastery of her fear. Jeanne would then be taught preperformance relaxation techniques. She might also be taken through *systematic desensitization* to help further reduce her fear. To ensure future success while under pressure, a sports psychologist would guide Jeanne to use mental rehearsal so she could *practice staying calm*.

From this perspective, Jeanne's performance problem would take center stage, and all treatment would be aimed at eliminating her fears *in the present.* Unfortunately, attempting to resolve her problem in this way led to only *limited* and *temporary* results. Why?

Because Jeanne's fear was not being consciously generated by her focus of concentration or her negative self-talk. These were merely *conscious symptoms* of unresolved physical and emotional traumas from early in life. *To not understand Jeanne's trauma history is to not understand Jeanne's performance struggles, and without this understanding, successful resolution of her RSPP was impossible.*

This became clear when Jeanne was taught several cognitive-behavioral focusing and calming techniques for use before her competitions. Despite knowing what she needed to do to maintain composure, *she was unable to use these strategies* because the underlying traumas responsible for her fears weren't addressed. These traumas

Diagram/Table #6
TRADITIONAL SPORTS PSYCHOLOGY
vs.
BRAINSPOTTING SPORTS WORK

Traditional Approach	**Brainspotting Sports Work**
Uses cognitive-behavioral techniques (relaxation training, positive self-talk & affirmations, imagery, concentration techniques, reframing, etc.)	Uses Brainspotting and body-centered techniques

addresses unique physical and emotional roots of the problem within the athlete's brain & body

addresses conscious symptoms (excessive nervousness, low self-confidence, negative self-talk & doubts, negative imagery and faulty concentration)

focuses primarily on the athlete as a person and his/her unique trauma history and secondarily the athletic performance

focusing mainly on athlete's performance

leads to the complete resolution of the performance problem and conscious symptoms and to performance enhancement

leads to partial and/or temporary relief of symptoms

Traditional sports psych approach vs. Brainspotting Sports Work

were discovered during the personal and trauma history-taking that is a routine and integral part of our model.

Jeanne was the eldest of two girls born to her emotionally distant yet controlling alcoholic mother. Though fond of her father, Jeanne had limited contact with him, as his work kept him away from the family for extended periods of time. Her mother prohibited her from socializing with friends, so much of her early childhood was spent in isolation, except for the time she spent at the barn with the horses.

Mahala Rummell suffered panic in competition

When Jeanne was 13, she became increasingly interested in socializing, and her mother consequently refused to allow her out of the house except to go to school. Jeanne's only companion during this crucial developmental year was her horse, Alfie. According to Jeanne, "Alfie was my best friend in the world," and she spent countless hours riding, grooming, and talking to him. He was her world.

Jeanne's trainers all commented on her natural talent and potential to excel in riding, perhaps to an Olympic level. Unfortunately, her mother was too depressed and self-absorbed to notice her daughter's riding. Jeanne felt that her mother deliberately limited the time that she spent in the barn with Alfie.

Three incidents at the conclusion of Jeanne's 13th year dramatically shaped Jeanne's life. They sowed the seeds of her performance panic that emerged 30 years later. The first event involved her trainer, whom Jeanne described as abusive and cold. Unbeknownst to Jeanne and her trainer, Alfie had been purchased with an undiagnosed leg injury, which the previous owner had masked by heavily medicating the horse. After a few weeks in his new home, the horse began to experience leg pain as the effect of the drugs wore off. In discomfort, Alfie tossed his head whenever ridden. The trainer counteracted this by tying a pull rope around Alfie's nose that, when tugged, would prevent the horse from the dangerous head tossing.

Unfortunately, the rope increased the horse's pain, which led him to pull up short and rear. During one lesson, Alfie, in pain, abruptly stopped in front of a jump. Jeanne didn't want to force him, correctly sensing that something was wrong; however, her trainer grew increasingly impatient, yelling at Jeanne to pull hard on the nose rope to force Alfie to lower his head and do the jump. Jeanne reluctantly complied, and Alfie reared up, lost his balance, and fell on top of her. His hind legs then kicked out and grazed Jeanne's riding helmet. Although she suffered a mild concussion, leaving her dazed, she miraculously escaped more serious injury.

The experience was extremely traumatic for Jeanne, but not because she came so close to sustaining a serious head injury. She suffered intense guilt for pushing her injured horse to jump in pain, putting Alfie at risk. Two weeks later, her mother unexpectedly announced that the family was immediately moving to Europe, as Jeanne's father had gotten a new job. The girl was then informed that her beloved horse would be sold. When she said goodbye to Alfie a few days later, Jeanne was overcome by grief and dread regarding her best friend's fate after they moved. As the family left, Jeanne was told to never discuss Alfie again. "Kids were not supposed to have feelings in my family," she explained.

Jeanne spent her 14th year in Switzerland, riding three or four times a week. Right before the family returned to the US she had a traumatic experience with her Swiss trainer. Despite Jeanne's scary spill on Alfie, she had not developed fear of riding. Over the years, she had become skilled at "stuffing" her feelings. One day, however, she was unable to do so when her trainer insisted that she challenge a four-foot jump, a height that she had never attempted before. Jeanne's trainer became progressively angry and abusive as Jeanne's fear bubbled up and immobilized her for the first time. The trainer suddenly cracked a large whip on the horse's rear, forcing the horse to fly over the jump carrying the terrified girl. Jeanne was profoundly disappointed in herself, as this incident broke her self-image as a relaxed, confident rider.

After returning home to the US, Jeanne's father lost his job and her mother became depressed and suicidal. The family had less money for Jeanne's riding, and she was forbidden to get a job at the barn to pay for riding expenses. With the family in turmoil and her mother more controlling than ever, Jeanne gave up her dream of riding competitively. *She didn't mount a horse again until she was 47. When she finally returned to the riding she had once so deeply loved and purchased her own horse, she was confused by the fear and guilt that surfaced.*

Mahala overcame her fears

In the light of her history, Jeanne's presenting problems made sense. We helped her work through the traumas including her fall with Alfie, having to say goodbye to her "best friend," her loss of courage in Switzerland at the hands of an abusive trainer, and the long-term impact of a cold and distant alcoholic mother. In response, Jeanne's fear and guilt began to subside. *When processing through these traumas was completed, Jeanne emerged guilt-free, able to ride confidently and even jump in competition without any fear whatsoever.*

Many parents, coaches, and sports psychologists mistakenly believe that they can make sense out of an RSPP by simply examining the athlete's *recent* performance history. An assumption is often made that there must be a direct relationship between the problem and something specific that *recently* happened to the athlete on the court, on the field, or in the gym. Although this is occasionally the case, usually it's not. This is why the athlete's trauma history *both in and out of his or her sport* must be closely examined to understand and resolve the performance difficulty.

A final example of the struggling athlete's need to be seen as a person with a personal trauma history is the story of Stacey, a 14-year-old level-7 gymnast. She was referred to us because of her fear of going backward on the balance beam. Stacey had stopped doing her back walkover on beam two years before. Her fear had more recently spread to backward moving skills on two other events. The young gymnast was terrified that she would fall off the beam, hit her head, and sustain a serious injury. Her fear of back walkovers had mysteriously appeared shortly after she had mastered the skill as a level-5 gymnast. During warmup, Stacey's coach spotted her for the first few moves, but when Stacey went to do her beam routine, she panicked, realizing she would have to do the back walkover without a spot. Despite her intense fear, she was able to force herself to go for the skill; however, as she put her right hand down on the beam, her hand slipped and she fell. An instant before her head hit the beam, Stacey managed to get her left hand down and push herself away before getting injured. This close call left her badly shaken, convinced that if she attempted another back handspring, she would miss and hit her head on the beam.

Over the next year, Stacey refused to go for the skill. On the rare occasions when she mustered up the courage to try, she invariably ended up reinforcing her fear by falling, yet two years later, she finally recovered the back walkover at a gymnastics camp and was able to comfortably execute it for almost the entire competitive season. One week before her level-6 sectional end-of-season meet, however, she

Lauren Cartmell competing at level 9, 2010 States in Colorado

inexplicably began to balk again as her fear became incapacitating. Since that time, she had been too terrified to attempt the skill.

Stacey's fear and immobility left her frustrated because the back walkover was a basic skill that she was capable of doing, but no matter what she tried or how angry her coaches got at her, she couldn't get her body to go for it. Stacey's trauma history in the gym was relatively limited. Although she'd had a number of close calls, she'd never suffered any serious injuries. Around the time she began balking again, she was badly shaken up on a backwards fall off of the bars. Beyond this incident and a few other scary but harmless near misses, the gymnast had never really been traumatized. Something else seemed to be fueling her fears.

When we looked more closely at Stacey's trauma history, we found several significant events that we believed were fueling her unconscious fears in the gym. Stacey's father was described as a physically and emotionally abusive man who abandoned the family when she was two years old. *Around the time that she was first learning the back walkover, her mother suffered a brain aneurism.* On the way to the hospital, Stacey was told to say goodbye to her mother. She was convinced that her mother was dying. Miraculously her mother survived. Stacey remembered *looking down at her unconscious mother* just before the EMTs put her in the ambulance. Stacey had never talked with *anyone*, including her mother, about her intense fears from this experience. It wasn't until we began to process it *two and a half years later that she shared it for the first time*. A year after the aneurism, Stacey's favorite uncle died, and her memory of the loss **was *looking down at him in the open casket*** as she said goodbye.

As we processed these incidents, it became clear that a good deal of Stacey's fears on the balance beam were *unconsciously connected* to the trauma of almost losing her mother. These fears were further fueled by Stacey's intense worries that if she hit her head on the beam, she too might die like her mother almost had. Stacey's case illustrates how traumatic experiences are frozen in the brain, including the images, emotions, physical reactions, and negative thoughts of the original experience. As previously discussed, when an athlete is reminded of the original traumatic experience, or is simply under stress, components from the trauma are unconsciously triggered and interfere with present performance. This is what happened to Stacey when she *stood on the high beam and looked down.* This vantage point on the beam unconsciously triggered the frightening image and body position of looking down on both her dying mother and her dead uncle.

Without an understanding of how the brain stores trauma, as well as an awareness of Stacey's personal history, it's impossible to understand the nature of her block on beam. Thus, without directly targeting and processing through the trauma-based roots of her block, it would have been impossible to help Stacey overcome her fear of the back walkover. Approaching her block by focusing on the fear and trying to teach her conscious techniques to get beyond it would have been like trying to stop a charging elephant with a pea shooter.

In the next chapter, "Amanda's Story," we will further illuminate the trauma basis of RSPPs and how resolution of these performance blocks requires careful examination of the specific underlying physical and emotional upsets. Amanda's case reflects both the limitations of traditional sports psychology and the power of Brainspotting Sports Work in resolving previously "irresolvable" performance blocks. In addition, we will begin to outline the healing process we take athletes through to help them free their brains and bodies from the debilitating effects of past physical and emotional injuries.

CHAPTER 6

AMANDA'S STORY
Overcoming Incapacitating Fears

Our ground-breaking approach to RSPPs can be illustrated with the story of Amanda, a level-9 gymnast blocked by fear. It was Amanda's case that convinced me (AG) of the unique power of Brainspotting Sports Work in resolving RSPPs.

Amanda was a talented and hardworking gymnast brought in by her mother. Amanda's intense fears had recently spread to "everything that I do in the gym." The 15-year-old athlete was passionate about gymnastics, which she had begun at age five, and dreamt of earning a Division I scholarship. She was intelligent, self-motivated, and goal-oriented. She was described by both her coach and mother as a perfectionist who was hard on herself when things went wrong.

Until Amanda, I did what all sports psychologists do: superficially attack the athlete's fears, self-talk, and concentration. I started by focusing on *pre-* and *in*-performance self-talk and concentration and followed with teaching conscious techniques to correct both. I was unknowingly working with the *conscious symptoms* of the problem rather than the *underlying causes*.

In the past, I had treated athletes with fear-of-injury–based blocks, especially those from inherently dangerous sports like gymnastics, skating, and diving, with marginal success. My frustration, coupled with my belief that I was missing something important, led me on a search for answers. Ultimately I discovered my co-author's work with EMDR and PTSD. His theory was that *all RSPPs had a trauma base*. He taught that

Amanda Dearman in competition

unless these deeper causes were directly addressed and worked through, the athlete *could not experience lasting relief.* This intuitively made sense to me. I had found the missing piece to the sports-performance puzzle.

Like many gymnasts her age, Amanda had her share of fears as she progressed through the ranks. For a short time at level 6, she had been afraid of back-tucks on floor and couldn't do them for a month. At level 7, she had developed a fear of tick-tocks on beam, forcing her to replace the skill. At level 8, she had suddenly balked on back giants on bars. This fear made no sense until it was discovered that Amanda was suffering from a pinched nerve in her neck. This caused loss of strength in her right hand, making it impossible for her to grip the bars as she swung. Although the impingement was corrected, her fear of back giants persisted and she couldn't bring herself to attempt them. An accident the following October elevated her fear to a potentially career-ending level.

Amanda had been doing straddle backs on bars during practice and was feeling confident. (A straddle back is a release move in which the gymnast flies backward from the high bar and then catches the low

105

bar.) This was Amanda's first day working on them without an extra mat underneath her, and her first turn was flawless. Although her second one was shaky, she recovered enough to pull it off. On her third attempt, however, things suddenly went very wrong. As Amanda swung to high bar, she noticed that something inside of her didn't feel right. She heard a voice in her head warning, "Don't go!" and instinctively decided to not do the giant. She casted over and began to fall, realizing in a panic that she had too much swing to stop her momentum. Instead, she flew over the bar, completely missing both hands. Amanda reflexively extended her arms, bracing for the impact.

The landing was horrific, bringing the entire gym to a hushed standstill. Amanda dislocated both elbows and broke her right arm in three places. The break required extensive surgery, and there was a serious question whether Amanda would ever be able to do gymnastics again. It took her 9 months and many painful hours of physical therapy before she was medically cleared to go back to the gym. Psychologically, however, Amanda's struggles were just beginning.

When cleared to return to the gym without restriction, Amanda was immediately plagued by fears. She was "gun shy" on bars, and her fears and tentativeness spread to beam, floor, and anything involving moving backward. During her rehab and for months after returning to the gym, she used the traditional sports-psychology techniques she found in two of my earlier books. Through hard work and tenacity, she slowly began mastering her fears and gradually recovered her "lost" skills. By the following October, a year after the accident, she had controlled her fears and was consistently going for all her skills. Amanda's coach reported that she had made great strides mentally and had beaten the odds by her amazing comeback.

Upon cursory examination, one could marvel at Amanda's miraculous return and tout it as a "happy ending" to a painful ordeal. Her fears had been successfully tamed and her mental toughness, honed by disciplined use of conscious sports-psychology techniques, had helped her return to pre-accident form.

Unfortunately, our gymnast's gutsy "triumph" would eventually prove to be *temporary* at best. Why? The underlying causes of Amanda's

Amanda competing the event in which she was injured

fear and performance blocks, her past physical and emotional trauma, had not been addressed at all. When an athlete's performance problem is no longer visible, that doesn't mean it has been resolved. Amanda was suffering from *sports* PTSD, but she, her coaches, and her parents didn't have a clue.

In December, on the eve of her level-9 competitive season, Amanda threw a double full on floor, an event in which she had *never* experienced any fear. Inexplicably, she froze in the middle of her round-off and landed hard on her back. Although it only knocked the wind out of her, she was badly shaken and too frightened to attempt any others that day. All of the hard work invested in mastering her fears and in mentally bouncing back were erased in an instant.

A few days later, Amanda had a nightmare in which she relived her bars accident. The nightmare was a classic flashback common to sufferers of PTSD, though flashbacks usually occur when one is awake. Amanda saw herself doing a front tumbling pass on floor, fighting with a voice in her head that cautioned her not to go, when a young gymnast

Nightmares are a part of STSD

directly crossed her path. In the dream, Amanda jumped to the side to avoid a collision. She extended her arms, bracing for the landing, and on impact broke both her arms.

Amanda awoke from the dream with a start, shaking uncontrollably. It took her more than an hour to calm herself and fall back to sleep. When sleep finally returned, however, her nightmare continued. Amanda was now on beam, doing the second back handspring of a combination, and she missed both of her hands. Before her head hit the beam, she awoke in terror, noticing that her toes were numb. Amanda stared up at the ceiling in a state of panic, hearing her heart pounding. It took a few moments for her to realize that it was *only* a dream, as the experience had felt so real. This blurring of reality and imagination is an indicator that this experience was a classic flashback. Amanda was too frightened to go back to sleep for the rest of the night.

The vivid nightmares opened the floodgates of her fears. All the doubts and trepidations that she had worked so hard to overcome flooded back into her consciousness with overwhelming force. In response to this panic, Amanda unknowingly slipped into a freeze state so common to trauma survivors. She went to the gym the next day and was too terrified to attempt anything. Her fears instantaneously spread to even the most basic skills in every event. There was little she could do without fearing she was going to get badly injured again. She left practice early, discouraged and in tears. The next day wasn't any better and ended the same way.

Amanda's panic was exacerbated by the closeness of the competitive meet schedule and her impatience with herself. How was she ever going to be able to compete while feeling this way? How could she possibly reach the lofty goals that she had set for herself in the season? She tried to steel herself to be strong and just go for things, but another part of her wasn't budging an inch! The mental techniques that she had successfully employed to subdue her fears were now completely ineffective. Amanda couldn't stop her brain from replaying the vivid images of "what ifs," the worst-case scenarios that would befall her if she decided to throw any of her skills. The images were mixed with those from her original accident and haunted her throughout her day.

Amanda's fears spiked, and she struggled with going to practice. Her coaches were clueless as to how to help her. They couldn't even get her to do basic lead-ups. Amanda was distracted in school as her mind raced with fear and her inability to master it. She stopped eating and had trouble sleeping. Hopelessness set in, and for the first time in her life, Amanda considered quitting the sport. It was then that her mother contacted me.

Amanda's story is part of a "silent epidemic" we have discovered in every sport, but gymnastics is a unique sport, where fear is an integral part of the process itself. This fear can be traced to three things. First, in almost everything athletes do in the gym, they're asking their bodies to do the unnatural and defy gravity. Human beings were not designed to run at full speed and throw themselves through space, twisting and flipping in multiple rotations. As a species, we are naturally comfortable with our feet firmly planted on the ground. Consequently, there is always fear aroused by the process of challenging gravity, especially if your aim is to throw yourself backward in the process.

Second, a real and present danger of physical injury exists daily in the gym. As a gymnast progresses through the levels, the degree of skill difficulty rises, as do the chances of sustaining an injury and an emotional trauma. Third, it's impossible to learn new skills and improve old ones without making mistakes. This is critical to the learning process, as it provides the gymnast's body with feedback on what went wrong and what needs to be done differently the next time.

Fear is a constant companion of the competitive gymnast

In gymnastics, getting this kind of feedback can be both physically and emotionally traumatic. Slips and falls can scare or injure a gymnast, and over the course of a career, these mishaps happen daily. Every fall, regardless of its severity or whether in practice or competition, accumulates in the athlete's body. Although most of these falls are shaken off and forgotten by the athlete, the body's memory of them is not. When a body memory is triggered by pressures, falls, or close calls, a performance fear or block can emerge, seemingly out of nowhere.

Because of the nature of the sport, fear is a constant companion of the competitive gymnast. Whether it's fear of a release, going backward, a new vault, or a dismount, the unexpected emergence of a fear or block can kill an athlete's joy, drive a coach to distraction, and confound the athlete's parents. As we see with Amanda, fear also can re-traumatize a gymnast and freeze her in her tracks. Fear is one of main reasons talented athletes prematurely leave this sport.

On a superficial level, there is a basic strategy for overcoming any fear: Confront the thing that you are most afraid of repeatedly, and your fear will diminish. Avoidance, in contrast, feeds our fears, causing them to intensify and spread. The stronger a fear gets, the more tendency there is to avoid it. In this way, avoidance sets into motion an escalating cycle of ever-increasing fear. Intellectually understanding how this fear cycle works is not enough by itself to stop it, however; knowing we have to go at our fears doesn't make doing it any easier. When fears are fed by underlying trauma, as they often are, consciously trying to force oneself to move toward them becomes impossible. Why is this so?

When an athlete has been physically and emotionally traumatized like Amanda was, her body remembers the entire experience in exquisite detail. The sights, sounds, physical sensations, and even smells of the trauma get locked in the athlete's brain and body. When that athlete is exposed to a reminder, usually unconscious, of the original incident, feelings from it are triggered, interfering with the performance of the moment. This is what happened when Amanda fell in the middle of her double back. The fall triggered body memories of her bars accident the previous year, and all the old fears returned in full force.

Because the original trauma is still "stuck" in the athlete's brain and body, she automatically operates in a self-protective mode. The brain and body respond as if the athlete is still in the same physical danger she was in at the time of the injury. It is impossible for the athlete to consciously override this powerful, self-protective reflex. This is why Amanda found herself helpless in the face of her fears and unable to force herself to attempt any skills. Her innate self-protective response wouldn't allow her to expose herself to further risk.

Amanda's injury history was more limited than that of Calder, the college pitcher discussed in Chapter 4; only two significant physically traumatic events formed the foundation of Amanda's performance difficulties. The primary one was the serious fall she suffered on bars. The second, a pinched nerve in her shoulder, had occurred 11 months prior. Although this injury wasn't a significant traumatic event, the resultant loss of strength in her hand made it impossible for her to swing on her back giants.

Initially, Amanda's complaints that she couldn't grip the bar and her fear that she'd fall were seen as a minor psychological issue with this skill; however, when she awoke one morning with no feeling in her right hand or arm, her parents realized that something physical was occurring and that she lacked the strength to hold on to the bars. A

Diagram/Table #7
HOW PAST TRAUMA GETS RETRIGGERED IN THE PRESENT

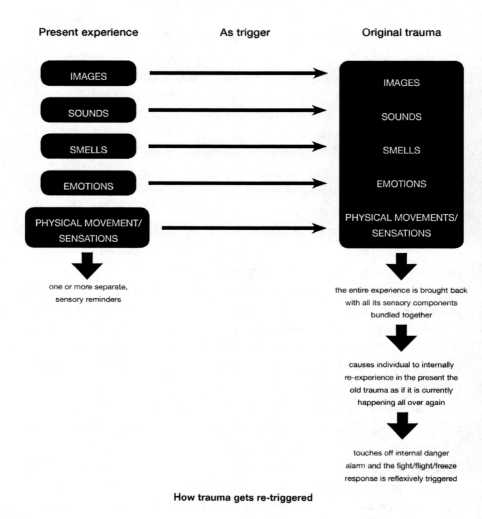

How trauma gets re-triggered

two-month regime of physical therapy corrected this problem so she was able to regain her grip strength. Despite this, her fear of the skill remained.

It's not only the athlete's history of sports injuries that makes her more vulnerable to the emergence of an RSPP; it's also related to the athlete's exquisite attunement to her body and the sense that something may be amiss. The voice in a gymnast's head that says, "Don't go," is often more a voice of *wisdom* than fear, correctly sensing that something is not right inside.

Amanda's fear of bars was also unconsciously fed by a number of other, less eventful, falls. These occurred while she was learning tick-tocks on beam, a skill that she was afraid of from the very beginning. She was sure that she would miss her feet and get seriously injured. Nothing had happened to her before and she had never witnessed any gymnasts falling on *this* skill; however, two months before her pinched nerve, Amanda had seen a close friend plant her face on the bar during a dismount, breaking her cheekbone. Vivid images of this had stayed with Amanda.

Despite the fact that Amanda was paralyzed by her fears and that those fears had generalized to every one of her events, her treatment was relatively straightforward. This was because of three factors. First, her trauma history was not extensive, and despite the fact that her bars accident was so traumatic, it was one isolated event. (If a performance problem results from a single trauma, it is usually much easier to work through than multiple traumas.)

Second, the ability of the athlete to overcome her problem is influenced by the coach's attitude. Those who respond to an athlete's repetitive performance problems with impatience, humiliation, and emotional abuse further traumatize the individual. This *always* makes the RSPP more intractable and complicates the treatment process. Fortunately, Amanda had a kind, supportive coach genuinely interested in her emotional and physical well-being. The coach didn't personalize Amanda's difficulties as a reflection of her own coaching inadequacy; she welcomed my input regarding how to help Amanda navigate the waters of her incapacitating fear.

Third, Amanda didn't suffer from any underlying psychological disorder. Helping an athlete work through fear and blocks is more complicated if the individual is clinically depressed or has an anxiety disorder. If an athlete suffers from depression or an anxiety disorder, she will be more vulnerable to developing an RSPP, and the working-through process will be more complicated and time-consuming.

Amanda's greatest vulnerability was her ***perfectionism***. She carried high expectations and was hard on herself whenever she fell short. When she failed to meet her unrealistic expectations, Amanda sometimes felt discouraged and hopeless. Her impatience and self-directed anger were provoked by her self-imposed deadlines to overcome her fears in time for the upcoming competitive season. Unfortunately this kind of self-pressure leads to impatience and frustration in not meeting goals or deadlines and makes the problem worse. We will discuss in Chapter 7 how performance expectations tighten the athlete physically and mentally.

As a perfectionist, Amanda ignored the small but discreet gains that she made throughout our early work. She instead focused on still having fears or on her inability to throw ***all*** of her old skills. This gave her a negatively skewed picture of her actual progress. After our first few sessions, Amanda began to feel more relaxed in the gym. She attempted the skills she had feared and was more aggressive in their execution. Her coach noted these significant changes in Amanda's condition. As her fears held her back from throwing the skills she needed for the upcoming season, however, Amanda dismissed her gains: "If I can't do these skills now, then I'm just wasting my time!" This all-or-nothing approach generated frustration and self-anger.

To combat her perfectionism, Amanda had to learn to be a kinder inner coach to herself. ***Self-empathy*** is an attitude needed for success in sports. This is especially the case for those grappling with RSPPs. Self-empathy is the ability to restrain the critical self and replace it with self-understanding, self-acceptance, and forgiveness. These are antidotes to perfectionism. Responding in this way creates a feeling of safety vital to breaking through the fear and blocks. When we respond as Amanda did with self-attack, we increase our insecurity. This hypercritical response on the inside has a similar effect to an abusive coach on the outside.

In Amanda's initial sessions, we focused on "tuning down" her panic in the gym. We reduced her fear of reinjury by processing through her bars accident. We used state-of-the-art trauma techniques like Brainspotting to systematically process out the debilitating components of each of her stored traumas. This resulted in her no longer being continuously triggered every time she was exposed to the performance arena.

Amanda was clearly suffering from STSD. Her performance-disrupting anxiety resulted from **unconsciously stepping back inside** her original scary experience. Our treatment process aims at helping Amanda, and other athletes like her, establish emotional and bodily distance from athletes' sports traumas.

One element we target is anticipatory anxiety, fear that *"IT"* will happen again. Depending on the individual, the "it" can refer to reinjury, wildness on the mound, hitting the board on a dive, messing up in goal again, or simply being humiliated. In my treatment with Amanda, we systematically targeted her anticipatory fear of reinjury until it completely dissipated.

We work with anticipatory anxiety by having the athlete activate it by imagining his worst fear of what might happen. This draws out the unconscious fear by spiking the athlete's level of distress. Once this is accomplished, we ask the athlete to pinpoint where he feels the activation in the body. We then locate the eye position where the greatest activity is held. The theory behind this is that your eye position connects directly with where certain traumas are held in the brain; by finding these locations, we are then able to more directly work to release the activation around that trauma. We add in bilateral sound, to be discussed in Chapter 9, and then systematically process the distress out of the athlete's body.

This is how I worked with Amanda's long-held fear of tick-tocks. Her fear was of missing the beam and sliding down the side of the apparatus. As she mentally put herself in this situation, Amanda experienced a physical jolt of fear pulse through her body. As we continued processing this reaction, the jolt gradually diminished until she couldn't activate it. Amanda could then imagine herself doing tick-tocks on beam **with no activation**. When she pictured herself missing, she "saw" her foot slipping harmlessly to the side of the beam.

As we continued, Amanda's fears of reinjury dissipated. She progressively regained her lost skills. We continued to strategically target each of her past traumas, including the nightmares and her fears of specific skills. Amanda's confidence level in the gym continued to rise. Although her fears periodically flared up, they were no longer paralyzing and were quickly worked through.

Two months after the start of her treatment, Amanda competed in her first meet. She came in first in the all-around! The next month, she went to States, hoping to qualify for Regionals. During the first three of the four events, she stayed focused and relaxed and performed well. The uneven bars was her last event, and she felt confident. Unfortunately, Amanda had to wait a long time between her warmups and her turn. During this time, she was intimidated by some of her competitors' routines. As a result, she was unfocused and fell off the bars on her mount, a cast handstand. She quickly recovered, and the rest of her routine was flawless, including her straddle back, the skill that she had badly injured herself on the previous year, but when she went into her dismount, she inexplicably froze and couldn't release the bar. As a result, her bars score wasn't high enough and she just missed making the regional team.

Her recovery complete, Amanda triumphs

A brief recurrence of an old problem is not unusual in this kind of work. After further processing the experience and her disappointment, Amanda was quickly able to consistently execute her bars dismount without difficulty. During the next year, Amanda continued to improve and had additional traumatic exposure (watching other gymnasts get injured and hurting her back on a fall), and we processed them through. The following March, at States, she qualified for Regionals. *On the big stage, Amanda hit all four of her events, to come in second in the all-around competition.*

Our aim, however, is not to simply remove the athlete's fear or performance block. Beyond this, we want to leave the athlete more resilient than *before* the onset of his or her original difficulties. Our goal is to help the athlete consistently perform at a higher level. *The same techniques that remove blocks can be used to significantly expand performance, especially for the athlete who is performing well.*

As mentioned in the Introduction, being relaxed before and during performance is a prerequisite to success, regardless of the sport. Without the ability to stay calm under pressure, even the most talented and well-conditioned competitors falter. We help athletes develop this ability to stay calm in a very different manner than that utilized by traditional sports psychologists. They teach the athlete specific relaxation techniques, including progressive muscle relaxation, self-hypnosis, breath-control training, and guided imagery.

We at times integrate these traditional strategies with our own powerful and focused methods. In our Brainspotting Sports Work model, we help the athlete discover his or her innate capacity for relaxation. For example, Amanda spontaneously accessed an image of being in a hot tub, feeling relaxed. This picture was associated with the color yellow. Both were utilized by Amanda *on her own* whenever she needed to feel calm and relaxed. She took this *relaxation resource* a step further and filled her bedroom with the soothing color yellow. Whenever she went to practice or competed in meets, she made use of both her relaxation image and color to both calm herself and expand her performance. This was further enhanced by the bilateral sound.

In the next chapter, we will examine another piece of the RSPP puzzle: *performance expectations*. Athlete, coach, and parent expectations feed a variety of performance problems. When left unchecked, they can hopelessly trap athletes. Performance expectations can also slow the treatment process. This occurred with Amanda when her own expectations about the speed of her recovery impeded our work. It was only after she learned to keep her expectations in check that she made the breakthroughs that brought her all the way back and to a higher level.

Chapter 7

WHOSE SPORT IS THIS ANYWAY?
The Damage Caused by Athlete, Parent, and Coach Expectations

Danny completed his high school sophomore year pumped up. He had worked his way from the bench to starting point guard, leading his team to the state semifinals. He was named to the conference all-star team as well as honorable mention as all-state. He averaged 14 points, 5 rebounds, and 4 steals. He matured into a fine play-maker and team leader and attracted interest from Division I programs. In the end-of-season meetings, the coach expressed great expectations in Danny for the next season and beyond. He said that with Danny running the offense, the team had a shot at winning its first state title.

Danny entered the AAU (Amateur Athletic Union) season with excitement and a renewed commitment to the game. He began to believe he could compete at the next level. He hit the weight room and ran four miles five days a week to get himself into peak condition for his junior year. He wanted to prove to his coach and the scouts that he had what it takes to be a big-time college point guard.

Despite his enthusiasm and dedication, something was off with Danny's spring and summer AAU seasons. He played well in practice but wasn't the same player in games. He wasn't as sharp as in the previous season, frequently losing the ball and committing silly mistakes. His shot never felt right, and Danny couldn't get it to drop when it counted. As a result, Danny redoubled his efforts. Recruiting letters and emails trickled in over the spring and summer, reminding Danny how much was at stake. At the high school tryouts in November, Danny was determined to prove himself, yet he harbored worry that grew in the fall. Even though he was in great shape, Danny was slower on the court and having problems with his ball-handling. He wasn't snagging his usual share of rebounds and was getting beaten off the dribble. His shot was still off, and this "new look" left his coach scratching his head.

Worse, the harder Danny tried, the more his game slipped. Although he easily made varsity, it was doubtful whether he was playing well enough to start. Skill-wise, Danny was the best point guard, but he just wasn't performing. He started the season opener and seemed out of control. In the second half, the coach benched him after his fourth turnover. Danny was reinserted with three minutes left and was a non-factor in the team's close win.

Danny predictably drove himself harder. His practices reflected his sense of urgency. He continued to commit errors and got progressively less playing time. As he saw his season and big dreams heading south, he got down on himself.

Danny didn't have an extensive injury history like many of the athletes we see, but he did have *enough* traumatic experiences in athletics and in his life to be vulnerable to RSPPs. Danny's expectations of having an outstanding year triggered the emergence of his performance difficulties. His story illustrates the destructive power of expectations and their role in disrupting performance and exacerbating preexisting performance problems.

Expectations refer to aspects of performance related to *outcome* and the *future*—in other words, anticipating how the tryout, performance, or season will turn out. "Will it be a success or a failure? Will I get reinjured? Will Coach think I'm good enough to start?" Expectations are closely related to goals, but goals focus on what the athlete *wants to have happen.* By contrast, expectations carry the seeds of anticipatory anxiety and so focus on what the athlete is *afraid might happen.* Let's examine the differences between the two.

Goals are essential for ultimate success. They give training focus, channeling efforts purposefully. Goals map out the athlete's future with an emotionally compelling desired outcome. Goals answer the question, "Why am I putting myself through all of this hard work?" Without clear, compelling goals, training often becomes diffused.

Unfortunately, many coaches and athletes use goals incorrectly. They fail to understand that *goals are a training tool for use in practice. The sole purpose of goal-setting is motivation, not pressure.* Problems emerge when athletes take their goals into competition. This takes them out of the moment and thus can create performance difficulties. Outcome goals taken into performance become expectations and, as a result, become destructive.

Expectations can sink performance

Expectations, like goals, are both future- and outcome-oriented. They relate to what we anticipate will happen in practice, competition, or the season. On the surface, expectations seem similar to goals. On closer examination, however, they prove to be far from that. When *used appropriately,* goals are constructive motivational tools that organize, orient, and provide meaning to our *practices.* Expectations, in contrast, involve an inherent pressure and create a sense of *urgency.* They attach an over-inflated importance to performance and so create *internal conflicts.* Athletes experience this conflict as **"I need to," "I have to,"** or **"Oh no, what if I don't?"** Future-directed self-talk tightens athletes' muscles, undermines their self-confidence, and distracts them from the task at hand.

The athlete's focus on what is *going* to happen is analogous to the self-protective orienting response found in all animals. As discussed in

Chapter 3, the orienting response involves vigilant, continuous scanning for potential signs of danger in the animal's environment. When the animal senses a potential threat, it **turns toward** the threat, poised for fight or flight if necessary. The animal responds **as if** a life threat is imminent. It doesn't relax and return to its normal behavior until certain that the potential danger has passed.

How does the orienting response play out for athletes? When we hear an unexpected sound, we reflexively turn, or orient, in its direction with the **expectation** of responding to the cause of the sound. Similarly, athletes' expectations entail a special kind of orienting response, or turning toward, a potential threat; however, the "danger" that athletes reflexively respond to is on the **inside**. It's their internal conflict of meeting expectations and the fear that they may fail to do so.

Fear is at the core of STSD

When we examine athletes' expectations, we find **fear** underlying those expectations. Sometimes the fear is of physical injury or reinjury. More often, expectations are the fear of failure, both conscious and unconscious. Failure followed by humiliation represents the heart of the athlete's "danger." Although the athlete's survival is not at stake, emotionally, there is the "life threat" saying, "If I fail, I will be humiliated and destroyed." The expectation that a botched performance will result in humiliation triggers the survival response, which results in negative performance.

This happened when golfer Scott Hoch stood over a two-foot putt on the first playoff hole at the 1989 Masters. His thinking was fueled by his expectation of winning. Under normal circumstances, a professional golfer makes this putt over 95% of the time, but Hoch had other things on his mind. He spent two minutes over the putt, looking at it from every angle, anticipating every possible break. The longer he waited, the more he thought and the further away he got from his natural instincts.

When Hoch finally stepped up to the ball, he backed off, unable to decide whether to play the break soft or firm. When he stepped back in, a final thought ran through his mind: "This is for all the marbles." Hoch hit the ball firmly, sending the ball five feet past the hole. He regained his composure and made the comeback putt, forcing a second playoff hole, but he eventually lost to Nick Faldo.

Hoch's overthinking and outcome focus revealed his expectations of winning and his underlying fear of losing. Because of these expectations, he injected pressure into what could have been a routine putt. Without expectations, Hoch would have gone on automatic with a relaxed focus on the ball as he putted.

Was Hoch *consciously* aware of the "danger" that he was "orienting toward"? Did he sense the negative consequences attached to failure as he endlessly stood over the ball? Did he *consciously* worry about the humiliation that would greet him if he missed the easy putt? Whether or not he was conscious of the "danger" is unknown. The results suggest that negative expectations were playing on his mind. How else can we understand a seasoned pro spending so much time over a routine putt and then missing it so badly? Ironically, the fear of humiliation that was likely lurking in his mind delivered exactly that outcome. For years after this event, the sports media wouldn't let Scott forget his meltdown: "Scott Hoch rhymes with choke."

Athletes' expectations are actually *conditioned reflexes*. For example, a baseball player who has been beaned becomes afraid of getting hit in the head more than of anywhere else on his body. The trauma conditions his reflexes to respond self-protectively *whenever* he steps in at the plate. As a result, he is distracted, tense, and back on his heels. This trauma-conditioned *survival* response always interferes with the athlete's response as it is conditioned into muscle memory. This is what happened to Scott Hoch when he finally executed his ill-fated putt. A conditioned survival reflex short-circuited his natural reflexes, which would have allowed him to easily sink the putt.

In resolving RSPPs, we focus on the trauma-conditioned reflexes to **decondition** them. That is, **we undo the interfering survival reflexes,** allowing the athlete to relax and let his or her naturally developed performance instincts take over. Our method helps us locate, process, and then release these trauma-conditioned responses. The batter who has been hit in the head no longer expects this to happen again when he digs in at the plate. He is able to relax and let his muscle memory take over. The gymnast who sustained a serious injury on her release move on bars now effortlessly executes this move. The skier who suffered a severe knee injury during a race is now able to go all out instead of sitting back on his skis. A golfer is able to putt free of the expectation that his wrists will freeze and jerk, leading to an errant three-footer.

This is seen in the **let's-see-what-happens** attitude, which is diametrically opposed to the **what –if-"IT"-happens** expectation. When you go into a performance without expectations, the emotion that usually emerges is **pleasant surprise,** but when you carry expectations into important performances, the emotion that arises is one of **bitter disappointment.** When you emerge with disappointment, it's a clue that you carried in the pressure of expectations.

It's important to distinguish anticipation from expectation. Expectations are a conscious product of the thinking front brain, while anticipation is more an unconscious product of the deep brain. Anticipation is something that great athletes automatically do that is instinctual. When athletes anticipate, they unconsciously intuit ahead into the immediate future. They anticipate the movement of the defender or the flight of the ball a split second before it actually happens. This uncanny ability to "know" what will happen next is found in great athletes. When you anticipate in this way by **feel,** you succeed; however, when you anticipate with **thought,** you fail.

Yankees shortstop Derek Jeter frequently displays this instinctive ability to know where the ball will be hit. Contrast Jeter's anticipation to that of former teammate second baseman Chuck Knoblauch.

Knoblauch was a gold-glover on the Twins, but after a trade to the Yankees something went wrong. After a series of embarrassing, well-publicized throwing errors, Knoblauch began to worry that "it" might happen again with every throw to first. As a consequence, his body instinctively mobilized itself for danger rather than baseball when he took the field. Jeter's anticipation was both instinctive and unconscious, aiding expanded performance. Knoblauch's expectation was conscious and stress-inducing, interrupting his natural performance.

SOURCES OF EXPECTATIONS

We have outlined how expectations fuel choking, slumps, and blocks, serving as triggers for the emergence of RSPPs. When athletes struggling with RSPPs are subjected to expectations to "hurry up and get over it," the RSPPs become more intractable. These expectations can be generated internally by the athlete, as in Danny's case, or can be fueled externally by coaches, parents, fans, or even sports psychologists. Without an awareness of the source of these expectations, the repetitive performance problem will usually continue and worsen. In contrast, awareness both of the source of these expectations and the expectations' destructive nature can reverse their negative effects.

ATHLETE-GENERATED EXPECTATIONS

Athletes in the clutches of RSPPs have little patience for their performance difficulties. The RSPP makes no logical sense to the suffering athlete. Why should a gymnast suddenly be unable to do a back handspring on beam, a skill she's been doing for years? Why should a diver be inexplicably terrified of his inward dive he learned five years before?

How is it possible for a second baseman to be unable to make a routine throw to first or for a swimmer to go much slower in races than in practice?

The illogical nature of performance problems fuels the athlete's impatience and frustration, leading to the expectation of quickly getting over the problem. Working harder and trying to will oneself through a repetitive performance problem *never* works. When athletes fail to turn the RSPP around, the response is predictable: They turn their frustration and impatience inward. They take on the role of a bad inner coach, putting themselves down by using negative self-talk, which further erodes their already shaky self-confidence.

For example, a level-10 gymnast who had sustained a serious injury doing a backward release move on bars eight months earlier couldn't get herself to go for back tumbling on floor. The more she struggled, the more frustrated she got with her inability to do a simple pass. Her impatience quickly turned into self-hate, and she beat herself up when she couldn't get her body to go for the tumbling. She was reduced to tears, ending the hope of a productive practice. Her expectation of quickly surmounting the problem was replaced by expectation that the problem would continue and worsen.

Carrying this negative expectation into a performance activates a self-fulfilling prophesy that ensures failure.

For example, a cross-country runner struggled with bouts of inexplicable exhaustion during races. The fatigue, which never happened in practice, overtook her during the second mile, causing her to get passed by teammates she dominated in training. She became highly anxious before races that "it" was going to happen. This kept her up the night before races, tightening her physically. When the race started, her tension and nervousness intensified, ensuring she'd run inefficiently and tire prematurely. The situation worsened as she approached the second mile. Her worries and thoughts of "here we go again" interfered with proper breathing, tightened her, and guaranteed she'd slow down. The runner's expectations of failure fed her RSPP.

An athlete's impatience and frustration with RSPPs are fueled by two character traits common to dedicated athletes: *perfectionism* and *competitiveness*.

PERFECTIONISM—"Perfectionists fail 100% of the time."

Perfectionism is the internal quest to be perfect in all endeavors, accepting no mistakes. It seems like an important trait for the serious athlete, but in truth, perfectionism exceeds the adaptive and the healthy. Ironically, perfectionism can be a cause of an athlete's failure. How is this possible? Perfectionism is a double-edged sword. If you control it, you can cut through obstacles and carve a pathway to success, but when perfectionism gets out of control, it turns against you, shreds your self-esteem, and ultimately kills your dreams.

Diagram/Table #8
THE DOUBLE EDGED SWORD OF PERFECTIONISM

The double edged sword of perfectionism

The problem with perfectionism is that it replaces striving for excellence with unrealistic intolerance of anything short of the unattainable. The inability to tolerate mistakes is a problem in sports because there is no such thing as perfection. By nature, we are flawed in our individual uniqueness. This is true in athletics as well as in the rest of our lives. Even in the best performances, there are always imperfections. *Sometimes a "perfect" performance still results in a loss!*

Mistakes and failures are inevitable in sports. It's how we handle them that really counts. Perfectionists cannot adapt to this reality. Their unrealistic expectations bypass their better judgment. They expect that every time they step up to the plate, they'll get a hit, that every shot they throw up will go in, and that in every competition, they'll emerge victorious. Although intellectually they know it's impossible, emotionally they respond to their failures as if it isn't impossible.

There's a distinction between *hating losing* and the *inability to tolerate it.* Dedicated athletes hate losing with a passion. They train hard to win and find losing distasteful; however, they have losing in perspective. They understand that failure is an inevitable part of competitive sports and a *necessary prerequisite* to success. They know failure provides feedback about what needs to be changed for a better result next time.

Perfectionists are unable to make use of these lessons. They are distracted by the unacceptability of failure itself. They get "emotionally hijacked" by self-directed anger, and these emotions blind the perfectionistic athlete, making it impossible for him or her to see the positive in the perceived negative of failure. A perfectionist distorts reality regarding his or her self-evaluation. The perfectionist is always his or her own worst enemy and harshest critic. What coaches or parents assess as a great performance is often viewed by the perfectionist as mediocre.

For example, a high school basketball player single-handedly carried her team through both the quarters and semi-finals of the state tournament. In the finals, she continued her dominant ways, scoring 28 points, keeping the game close. With five seconds left, she dribbled up court with her team down by two. Shaking two defenders, she pulled up for a three-pointer that could have clinched the game and state championship. The ball rimmed out and her team lost. She was inconsolable afterward, feeling like a complete failure. She blamed herself for the loss, believing she had let down her coaches and team. She even seriously considered quitting the game!

Athletes struggling with RSPPs have more difficulty getting unstuck if they are perfectionists. Perfectionism fuels the athlete's impatience, blinding him to the incremental gains that are integral to a successful treatment process. For example, a tennis player struggling with her serve had her best serving match in months but lost to an archrival. Her coach was delighted that she was finally able to relax and serve well. The player's interpretation: "She beat me, so my serve must still be messed up."

Another example is a gymnast afraid of executing a back walkover on beam. She discounted positive steps if she was unable to go for the move. She ignored the fact that her fear level had reduced so that she was able to do the skill on a floor beam. This false assumption of the perfectionist that ***nothing has changed*** ensures that he or she will remain stuck.

COMPETITIVENESS

Competitiveness is the second character trait that can fuel an athlete's difficulties and interfere with treating RSPPs. Like perfectionism, competitiveness is a doubled-edged sword. When wielded correctly, competitiveness can raise the level of the athlete's game and cut a path to his or her athletic dreams. Competing against stronger opponents improves the athlete's skills, challenging him or her to improve. Tough training partners keep athletes highly motivated, making their training more productive.

Seen through a healthy lens, competitors view opponents as "partners" in the pursuit of excellence. Opponents push us to better, faster, and stronger performances, increasing the chances of achieving our personal goals. Significantly, the meaning of competition from its Latin roots is "a seeking together."

When athletes lose control of the sword of competitiveness, it shreds their game and self-confidence. Overly competitive athletes view opponents as ***personal threats***. They are preoccupied with and distracted by what the

Oh, my God!!! Will ya look at the size of that dorsal fin!!! Are you sure he's just a guppy?!!!

competition is doing. ***Paradoxically, over-focusing on opponents cause athletes to lose to the opponents***. To improve the odds of beating opponents, ***athletes need to concentrate more on themselves and less on the opponents***.

Colin, our Division 1 soccer goal-keeper from Chapter 2 struggling with panic between the posts, couldn't stop comparing himself with his freshman rival. In practice, he continuously looked over at the other net to see how his teammate was doing and who the head coach was observing. Even in matches, Colin continuously distracted himself by comparing his play to his rival's. Colin's preoccupation with his teammate intensified his anxiety, distracted him from his job, and fed his low self-confidence. It wasn't until Colin was able to temper this over-competitiveness that he was able to resolve his performance problems.

EXTERNALLY GENERATED EXPECTATIONS: COACHES AND PARENTS

No one surrounding the athlete wants to see him or her struggle with an RSPP. The longer the RSPP goes on, the greater the toll it takes. Because athletes' identities are tied up in their sports, the emotional havoc that the RSPP wreaks spreads to other areas in the athletes' lives. The sports problem quickly colors their academic performance and personal lives. As the crisis intensifies, their parents and coaches mobilize in an attempt to turn things around. Unfortunately parent and coach "help" is not always supportive, as well-meaning parents and coaches can inadvertently "add fuel to the fire." The expectation trap that parents and coaches stumble into is a very common one: "Let's get them over the problem as quickly as possible." Although on the surface this may seem like a useful response, this performance expectation exacerbates the RSPP.

We are inclined as human beings to organize our lives to avoid pain and pursue comfort. The pain of an RSPP spreads from athletes to everyone surrounding them, catalyzing a frantic effort to solve the "riddle" and stop the discomfort. Coaches pull out every tool in their toolboxes to help athletes past their difficulties. They endlessly tinker with the athletes' mechanics; they increase the athletes' workloads or alter their practices. When these fail, the coaches may challenge the athletes to take control and *just do it.*

To the highly responsible coach, an underachieving athlete reflects that the coach is not doing his or her job well. A coach's ability is often judged in these narrow performance terms. Accordingly, coaches are vulnerable to experiencing athletes' repetitive performance problems as direct threats to their professional competence. When all of their interventions have been met by repeated failure, many coaches lose their patience and emotionally turn on the athlete.

For example, in 1987, when Mackey Sasser continued to triple pump the ball before throwing it back to the pitcher, one of his coaches called him out in front of the entire team. The coach told Mackey he would be fined $20 every time he failed to throw the ball back properly. Sasser was humiliated by this incident. Unfortunately, this kind of demeaning, expectation-fueled coaching response to an RSPP is common. In the end, it intensifies the performance woes as it retraumatizes the athlete, making him or her more self-conscious. Sasser told us that after this incident, his anxiety about throwing spiked.

Like coaches, parents get caught up in their children's performance problems. As a consequence, they inadvertently do more harm than good. Parental intervention is driven by a sincere desire to help the child. Watching your child repeatedly fail and suffer is a painful motivator for a loving parent. These parents often offer "helpful" suggestions aimed at resolving the RSPP; when the child is unable to solve the problem with this "help," however, these parents can become frustrated.

The parents' expectation that their child athlete get over the RSPP quickly comes from an inability to clearly understand it: How is it possible for my daughter to not be able to throw a back handspring when she's been doing them for years? Why can't my son get a hit in a game when he always belts the hell out of the ball in batting practice? Why is my daughter afraid of contact in her soccer games when she knows how to play this game so well?"

Parental involvement can work for or against the athlete

Sometimes the root of an RSPP can be traced back to parental expectations and pressure. When parents are more invested in the sport than in their child, the result is often a performance problem. For example, a 13-year-old figure skater was stuck on her double axel for more than a year. No matter what she tried, she was unable to get herself to relax enough to correctly land the jump. Her coach was confused because the skater had never experienced any performance problems during the learning process.

In meeting with both the skater and her mother, it became clear to us that skating was more important to the mother than to the daughter. Although the 13-year-old loved the sport, she wasn't interested in pursuing it to a national level. She was content competing locally and regionally. Her only stated goal for the sport was to have fun. Her mother, however, was distracted by the Olympic theme that played in her head. She believed that if her daughter worked hard enough, she could become a national or even Olympic champion. The girl's difficulty in learning her double axel stemmed directly from her mother's goals conflicting with her own. The expectation pressured her and unconsciously locked her up.

It's imperative that both parents and coaches remain in touch with the athletes' reasons for competing. Appropriate adults stay in tune with the athlete's goals. They allow these goals to guide their interactions with the athlete. In the process, parents and coaches need to be careful to keep their own goals and expectations out of the equation. When adults allow the young athletes this kind of psychological space, the athletes stay happier and more relaxed and are more able to overcome the RSPP.

This means that parents and coaches need to be patient and uncon-ditionally supportive of the athlete. They need to be sensitive to the ath-lete's plight and reassuring that the athlete will eventually be successful in working it through. Instead of expectations, patience and empathy from the important adults involved create a safe environment that is critical for athlete's working through RSPPs.

THE ATHLETIC CHAIN OF EXPECTATIONS

The athlete's self-expectations are at the end of a long chain of expectations found in organized sports. The athlete's self-imposed pres-sures are often fed by parents and coaches. The expectations that par-ents hold for their son or daughter are fueled by their own self-expectations to produce a successful child. When their child strug-gles performance-wise, parents feel that their child's failings are a reflection of their own failings.

Similarly, coaches have little tolerance for underachieving ath-letes, as they reflect on the coaches' competence. Their job security depends on producing "winners," and athletes who struggle with RSPPs aren't often successful. When their teams or athletes don't win, coaches fail to meet a wide array of implicit and explicit expectations. A losing team leads to unhappy parents, fans, and alumni. A losing pro-gram exposes the coach to the perception of failing in the eyes of his or her bosses, the program's athletic director and board of directors. When the coach doesn't produce a winning team in a "reasonable" period of time, his or her job may be in jeopardy.

The pressure the coach feels from the athletic director to produce is parallel to the pressure that the athletic director feels from his or her administration. The athletic director's mission is to develop and supervise a successful sport program, especially in the "more important" sports of football and basketball. Consistently mediocre teams are concrete "evi-dence" that the athletic director isn't doing his or her job.

In turn, the athletic director's "poor performance" reflects on the top academic administrators who are pressured by parents and alumni to keep their school competitive in the larger market. In college athletics, losing

Diagram/Table #9
THE ATHLETIC CHAIN OF EXPECTATIONS

alumni/fans/parents/peers/media

apply direct pressure on

school administration

college president, school board, superintendent, high school principal,

athletic director

team's head coach

athlete and his/her performance

The athletic chain of expectations

sports teams mean unhappy alums, and unhappy alums are not generous alums. The college president understands the financial power of winning teams in relation to alumni donations and college recruitment, so even the president feels the pull to have a winning athletic program representing the university.

Consider the case of the University of South Carolina's football program. The Gamecocks gave head football coach Steve Spurrier a $500,000 raise, extending his contract through 2012. Spurrier's salary

was boosted to $1.75 million while the average salary at the university for a ***full tenured professor was $92,000.***

As the chain of expectations filters down to the athlete, it intensifies each step of the way. Occasionally, an exceptional coach acts as a buffer, protecting athletes from the expectations that filter down this chain. Ex-Yankees manager Joe Torre is an example. Temperamental owner George Steinbrenner was a micromanager with high expectations and no tolerance for anything short of perfection. When his players and coaches didn't produce fast enough, he publicly criticized them and was quick to trade or fire them. The pressure he applied was intensified by the expectations and scrutiny of the New York fans and sports media.

When the Yanks lost the ALCS to their arch-rivals, the Red Sox, in 2004 after being one out away from sweeping them, Steinbrenner was ready to clean house from manager Joe Torre downward. The same dynamic reoccurred in the 2006 ALCS when the Yankees lost four in a row to the Tigers after winning the first game. In both years, Steinbrenner went public with his displeasure with his manager. Torre, however, did not pass on the pressure and expectations to his players. Instead, he buffered Steinbrenner's bluster and provided safety for his players.

All of us have performance expectations for ourselves; however, under normal circumstances, these expectations never reach the disruptive level of intensity seen with RSPPs. ***Athletes, coaches, and parents need to be mindful that performance expectations interfere with expanded performance and intensify RSPPs.*** Athletes translate these expectations into conscious thoughts like *I have to get a hit, I need to score 10 points,* or *What if I lose again?* As we've discussed, expectations lead to preperformance nervousness and block athletes from playing to their potentials.

Athletes translate these expectations into the voice of what we call the "inner critic," which then pops up during a hard race or tough practice: "This is too hard. I'm too tired. Why is everybody else doing better than me?" Self-talk is also frequently used as a vehicle to coach ourselves right before and during our performances: "You've got to calm down and make sure you keep the ball out in front of you. You've got to have good touches and look for the open space. Make sure you play clean and don't foul."

It is believed that when kept positive, self-talk is a useful, self-confidence–building tool. In traditional sports psychology, self-coaching with "positive affirmations" is an important mental skill to be developed. *Unfortunately, even when positive, self-talk is conscious and potentially performance-disrupting*.

For athletes struggling with RSPPs, there appears to be a constant internal battle between "good" and "evil." Athletes try to maintain positive self-talk about their upcoming performances, but their minds are infiltrated by negative, pessimistic voices: *What if it happens again? What if I can't throw the ball back to the pitcher? What if I balk again? What if I get sick before my race again?*

With athletes struggling with RSPPs, underlying anxiety deriving from past traumas feeds negative expectations. This negative internal process sets up the athletes for exactly what they are trying to escape: more performance problems. In the next chapter, we will more closely examine self-talk, its relationship to RSPPs, how it works against us, and *how we can learn to use it to our advantage*.

CHAPTER 8

SELF-TALK AND REPETITIVE SPORTS PERFORMANCE PROBLEMS
The Battle That Rages Within—The Voices of "Good" and "Evil"

For athletes struggling with RSPPs, the battle starts the moment they know they'll have to perform. It could be the night before that big game, race, or competition. It could start an entire week before. Once they realize they will be put in *that* situation *again*, the anxiety gradually builds. It is fueled by an increasing dialogue in the athlete's head. The struggle is between the positive and the negative, and between desperate hope and intense fear. A huge battle of wills is raging between two different parts, which many of our clients have described as the *angel* on one shoulder against the *devil* on the other.

Self-talk can be negative or positive

On the positive side, athletes try to desperately reassure themselves that they're absolutely ready, that they have the skills to get the job done, and that everything will turn out fine. Athletes may remind themselves of all that they've accomplished in an attempt to present a compelling case for the positive. This side also offers "helpful" last-minute performance strategies and coaching on proper technique. On the negative side, athletes won't let themselves forget subpar, embarrassing performances. The negative side runs through "what if" laundry lists of everything that could go wrong, leaving them paralyzed with self-doubt. Part of this negativity stream involves an urgent review of all the things they *shouldn't* do.

The internal battle is classic: "You *can* do this! I know you can. Practices have been great. You're in great shape. Coach thinks you're ready. Just stay relaxed and use your skills." Before this self-talk takes root, negative voices begin to punch the positive arguments with gaping holes. Soon, the negativity is so resounding that it strikes fear in the athlete's heart and sends the positive thoughts fleeing like outmanned, retreating soldiers.

"I *hope* I play well, but *what if* I don't? *What if* I'm tentative again? Coach was angry with me. *What if* I play scared again? I shouldn't think about getting reinjured. I can't worry about losing the ball, but *what if* I do? I just wish I didn't have to play today. I have a bad feeling about this. I wish the game was over already."

The most common expression of the negative side is *"what if?"* The "what ifs" are often the precursor to something bad happening for the athlete. They are an expression of the athlete's imagination turned against him or her. Simply put, the "what ifs" are the core of the athlete's worry and the predictor of a dreaded outcome. "What if it happens again?" is an obsessive thought that athletes with RSPPs can't shake. Interestingly enough, you will never find anyone using the "what if'" expression in relation to something like, "What if I play well and we win? Then I might have to be the tournament MVP and we'll be forced to be the state champions. How awful will that be?"

Athletes with RSPPs tie up a tremendous amount of energy in this positive-negative whirlpool. Regardless of which side "wins," the internal conflict shifts the athlete into the conscious-thinking *front brain*. Overthinking then tightens the athlete's muscles and distracts him or her from his or her performance. The negative voice is *always* louder and more persistent than the positive voice, ultimately drowning it out. To the blocked athlete, the negative voice always seems to be more *familiar* and *truer* than the positive one. Why is this? Let's try a brief experiment.

Negative thinking tightens muscles; positive thinking relaxes them

Close your eyes and think back to the last time you did a *good* job in work, school, or practice. As you do, notice your reaction to this experience. How does it make you feel emotionally and physically? How strong are these responses? Now let your mind clear and repeat the exercise, only this time focus on a *bad* job. Once again, notice how this poor performance makes you feel now both emotionally and physically. What did you discover?

Most people who try this exercise report that although the positive experience felt good, it didn't seem as clear, powerful, or long-lasting as the negative one. In fact, when they reflected on the poor performance, it was more detailed and left them with stronger body feelings and negative emotions that persisted longer. Why is this so?

Perhaps it's part of the human condition, but our attention is naturally drawn away from where we feel good to where we feel discomfort. No one obsesses about how good they feel physically or emotionally. Instead, we tend to notice those things that don't feel right. You notice the headache far more than you notice the relaxation in your brow. You notice your throat only when it's painful to swallow.

Similarly, your attention is grabbed by the deadline hanging over you rather than the completed project in your rearview mirror. This seems to be the case in every aspect of our lives. When our cars run smoothly, we are oblivious to how quiet the engines are, but an unfamiliar knocking from under the hood draws our attention right away.

Traditional sports psychologists teach cognitive skills to help athletes fight the "forces of evil" and so turn these negatives into positives. Their approach believes that conscious thought determines what athletes feel in their bodies, directly affecting their athletic performance. The theory is that "what you think" before and during performances causes subtle but significant physiological changes and these reactions, in turn, dramatically affect timing, technique, and execution.

The negative words, the "devil on the shoulder," whisper into athletes' ears, systematically tightening their muscles, accelerating their breathing, and leaving their extremities feeling cold. And the consequences of these physiological changes are devastating performance-wise. Tight muscles limit flexibility, shorten follow-through, and throw off timing. Shallower breathing tires the athlete out prematurely regardless of conditioning level. Cold hands and feet interfere with the *feel* of the ball, water, or equipment so essential in every sport.

The heart of this traditional theory is that conscious thought ***primarily*** determines body experience and therefore quality of performance. There is an important relationship between thought, physiology, and performance, but ***conscious thinking is not the starting point of this process***. Conscious thought is ***not*** the first stop on this train ride and in fact arrives in the latter stages of the journey. This parallels the idea that performance problems don't ***begin*** when they present themselves to the athlete and those around them. Many factors in the athlete's brain and body affect performance ***long before*** conscious thought and the performance problem break into awareness.

For example, our reflexive survival mechanisms are wired to react first and fastest. The complexity and linear nature of thought ***always*** take more time than reflexes. Witness the pitcher who gloves a screaming line drive in front of his face and then looks at the ball in his glove in total amazement. "Did I do that?" The pitcher's pure survival reflex, not any consciously directed thought, enabled him to catch the ball.

An athlete's brain or mind can't be separated from his or her body. This mind-body duality artificially attempts to make sense of the roles that physiology, psychology, and conscious thinking play in athletic performance. We agree that sports is 90% mental, but it's important to remember that the brain, the seat of the conscious and unconscious mind, is *in the body* and *is directly wired* into every part of the body. What may seem strictly mental is directly tied into what's physical, and vice versa. It's an inseparable loop. For the brain to survive, it has to receive oxygenated blood from the heart and lungs; however, heart and lung functioning are monitored 24/7 by the brain itself.

We believe that everything starts in the body. This is especially true for athletes because sports are all about the body and its movement. Think about our theory that sports injuries and other traumas are at the root of all RSPPs. Injuries and other traumatic experiences are not fully processed and as a result get frozen or stuck in the athlete's body in specific physical locations directly related to the trauma, and events like these are locked in the body and simultaneously stored in part of the brain as well in the inseparable brain-body loop.

Sports injuries get locked in the brain and the body

For example, a gymnast who breaks her ankle falling off the balance beam during a back handspring unconsciously retains a body memory of the entire experience. Her body locks anticipating the feeling of the backward movement before the fall, the loss of balance, the fall and its impact, the ankle pain, and even the ensuing medical treatment. This experience as well as the fear, frustration, and related emotions are frozen in her brain and felt in her body. When the recovered gymnast is unable to go for the same skill, she is not consciously aware of the reason.

By utilizing positive self-talk, the gymnast tries to encourage, cajole, and coach herself to push beyond this innate recoiling; however, the fear-generated negative self-talk ("Don't go; you'll get hurt; you can't do this.") wins out eventually. *This is because underneath the negative internal chatter is a genuine sense of mortal threat, and trauma symptoms like excessive fear, anxiety, avoidance, hypervigilance, and an exaggerated startle response are a reflection of this survival mechanism gone awry.* When a batter instinctively ducks away from a pitch not close to his head, his malfunctioning survival mechanism supersedes all else, including the price of disrupted performance. The organism's safety and survival always take precedence. *Our negative self-talk flows directly from our instinctive attempts at self-protection.*

In this way, *negative* self-talk always has an underlying *positive* intention. Last-minute self-doubts express a deeper fear that if we proceed, we'll be placing ourselves in harm's way. Recognizing the positive intent of negative self-talk is a crucial first step in breaking out of performance problems. This understanding can allow us to relax and change our relationships with our "negative" self-talk.

Most athletes tighten up when the negative voices begin to play in their heads. They respond as if it's the voice of the enemy and begin to fight it. They try to argue with it or consciously blockade it with positives. Battling with this self-protective part of ourselves is always a losing venture that only increases internal stress and stuckness.

For example, when our gymnast's conscious attempts to overcome her fears were met with consistent failure, she became impatient with herself. This response increased her tension and generated more fears whenever she attempted the scary skills, making them virtually impossible.

The internal battles between positive and negative self-talk operate on a deep level and *are not* a conflict between good and evil. At the unconscious level, this is about staying alive and safe. *This is why positive self-talk is ineffectual in overcoming fear-driven negative self-talk.* The self-protective, instinctive part is not interested in conscious pleading or arguing from the "positive" part because its only concern is survival.

I'm calm...I'm calm...I can do this...
Why do I feel like I'm going to barf?!!!

Traditional sports psychologists ignore the *positive intent of negative self-talk*, focusing instead on bolstering the *positive self-talk*. They teach mental rehearsal, repeatedly exposing the athlete to the feared skills to *desensitize* the athlete's fears. Sports psychologists encourage athletes to use "positive affirmations" by repeating them, writing them down, and posting them around their rooms. Athletes are also encouraged to internally challenge the part by presenting evidence why it's now safe to do the skills.

All of these conscious strategies, even when religiously practiced, are limited in their effectiveness. Even if the gymnast we discussed experienced a lessening of her fear, these effects would only be temporary, eventually wearing off. *That's because all of the positive self-talk in the world won't work when you feel like you're standing on the tracks, facing an oncoming train.* That's where primal survival instincts take over: We immediately forget whatever we're supposed to be doing and reflexively run for our lives!

WE ARE MADE UP OF PARTS

In our discussion about the internal conflict between negative self-talk and fear from one side and positive self-talk and hope from the other, the implication is that we as people and athletes are made up of parts and these varied parts are where these inner voices emanate from. Does this mean that we're all suffering from multiple personality disorder? No way!

Our emotions reveal different parts of ourselves

Our bodies are made up of parts: systems, subsystems, organs, cells, and even molecules! Our psychological makeup mirrors this, as our personalities comprise different parts as well. Let's take our emotions as an example. Depending on the situation, a person's emotions span a wide spectrum of feelings. There are times when the person feels joy and times the person is subdued, sad, or even depressed. Sometimes someone is scared or angry, and at other times, the person is extremely confident or calm. Our varied emotions are like discreet parts of us: the happy part, sad part, angry part, scared part, etc. Some of these parts we find desirable, and others, we wish would simply go away.

Athletes can see a similar kind of division considering the different parts of their games. With certain aspects, they feel more confident, whereas with others, they feel less sure. For example, athletes may trust their defense more than their offense, or they may feel more confident going to their left than their right. There are times when they feel aggressive, and other times, shaky and tentative. In this way, we reveal our confident parts, aggressive parts, doubtful parts, tentative parts, and so on.

Usually, ours parts operate totally outside of our conscious awareness. How is this possible?

As human beings, most of our daily functioning operates outside our consciousness. The nonstop beating of our hearts or the filling and emptying of our lungs are wired to operate unconsciously. This same out-of-awareness functioning exists in most of our physical performances both on and off the field. When we walk down the street, talk with a friend, or ride a bike, we do not consciously instruct ourselves on the proper technique, balance, and timing of these activities. All of these functions are unconsciously monitored by our deep brains. Similarly, the best athletic performances happen when athletes are "playing out of our minds." Playing out of their minds occurs because the athletes are not consciously instructing themselves but are trusting their training and unconsciously allowing their muscle memory and spontaneity to take over.

A good way to understand the unconscious and its relationship to the conscious mind is the metaphor of a sports arena. When we sit indoors watching a basketball game, there are numerous things in our awareness. We see the teams warming up, hear the announcer on the loudspeaker, and smell the freshly made popcorn. Our immediate awareness of those things represents the conscious mind.

A sports arena is a metaphor of the mind

As we watch both teams do battle, however, some things that go on in the arena are outside of our awareness that are essential to the smooth running of the game. In fact, there's a whole universe of activity going on below the arena's main floor that we rarely see or think about. These activities and functions represent our unconscious minds.

In the sub-basement, the heating and cooling systems regulate the indoor temperature. The plumbing system allows clean water to flow into and waste water to flow out of the arena. Additionally, electricity flows from the basement through its network in the building, enabling the illumination of the court and the projection of the announcer's voice and helping the food vendors keep their products either hot or cold. But we remain unaware of all of these goings-on until something breaks down. If an electrical short turns off the lights and air conditioning, the effects are immediately obvious to everyone. It's at this point that a qualified person needs to go down into the sub-basement to locate and fix the problem.

The "unconscious" is like the sub-basement. Housed in it are all the experiences that we've had growing up, both good and bad. All emotional and physical memories of past traumas and athletic injuries are stored there. The premise of this book is that these traumas locked in the sub-basement form the underpinnings for all RSPPs, so the first emergence of yips, balking, or performance difficulty is not the actual beginning of the RSPP. Instead, these represent when the accumulation finally overwhelms the coping mechanisms and breaks through to conscious awareness. Mackey Sasser's throwing problem first emerged briefly in 1987 after a foul tip hit off his throwing shoulder. His problem remained relatively manageable and mostly invisible for three years until it overwhelmed him, but *the roots of his yips had been brewing for many years prior to 1987*. This is a dynamic that we see with *everyone* we work with.

Athletes who begin to struggle with RSPPs notice an inner battle between their hopes and fears. *It's this battle between positive and negative self-talk that is often the first signal that the performance problem is breaking out.* Athletes describe this negativity as bubbling up from the "back" (sub-basement) of their minds. The feeling can be so powerful that they can't shake it. These fears and doubts let the athletes know ahead of time that regardless of how hard they try, they will fail.

Besides the fact that these fearful, negative, doubting voices from the unconscious most often have an underlying positive intention, what else can we learn from them? Where do they originate from, and who is really speaking?

Very often, the inner voices of doubt and fear that we hear are very old and come from early in life. These voices originate from our interactions with the most important people we grew up with. Mother, father, siblings, and other caretakers are the first significant individuals in our lives. Frequently, what we hear in our minds reflects what we heard from these important influences, both good and bad. These voices are expressions of our deeper selves who have developed over a long time.

Support from mom and dad builds confidence and enhances performance

If our families treat us with kindness, compassion, and praise, we "internalize" these voices and treat ourselves this way as we mature. In fact, much of our positive self-talk derives from what we heard in those early interactions. If those early caretakers and individuals were consistently unkind, critical, and demeaning, however, then we learn to treat ourselves in that way. Thus, our negative self-talk has its roots in these earlier communications. Add to this our subsequent interactions with teachers, coaches, and teammates in childhood and adolescence and we see how our self-talk is reinforced. The perfectionist athlete probably grew up with a perfectionist parent, and her impatience with herself probably was reinforced by an impatient coach.

DEALING WITH "NEGATIVE" SELF-TALK

The chatter of negative self-talk doesn't have to sound the alarm and muster the troops for battle. ***Rather than adopt an adversarial relationship with this part of us, we need to learn to respond to it in a more curious, relaxed, and accepting manner.*** Our so-called "negative" self-talk is not the voice of the enemy. It is instead the voice of a friend who, although seemingly misguided, actually has a positive motive. This friend is actually looking out for our well-being and is trying to keep us safe, but we don't appreciate how it's going about it, especially when the byproduct is frustration and distress. We just don't want to waste valuable energy battling with this "negative" part.

We can fight or join our negative self-talk

In traditional sports psychology, the athlete is encouraged to battle with the negativity and replace it with "positive self-talk." The ultimate goal is to challenge and even banish the inner critic, but when we try to subvert the inner critic, it returns with even greater force. This is usually manifested in our bodies as increased anxiety, lack of coordination, and the freeze response. The dreaded performance yips represent the final stage in the critic's hostile takeover. The message is clear: "You didn't listen. You've left me with no other alternative than to shut you down!" What starts off as one wild pitch sailing over the catcher's head therefore ends up as the pitcher not being able to throw the ball 20 feet in a short toss.

We encourage getting into the habit of **simply noticing** negative self-talk and understanding that it's motivation goes beyond the anxiety-generating words in your head. If we release the adversarial role and listen to it with **openness,** we begin to understand that the internal chatter is an expression of the body desperately trying to get our conscious attention.

This is an example of the back-and-forth internal dialogue that used to go on in the mind of Calder, the college pitcher from Chapter 4:

Critic (after throwing a wild pitch): You suck!

Self: What?

C: You heard me! You suck! You blew it!

S: Screw off!

C: You suck, and you're going to do it again. I just know it!

Self tries to shut the voice out and focus on throwing the next pitch, which is even wilder than the first.

C: You see. I told you that you'd do it again! You are *so* bad! How did you even make this team?

S: Shut up!

C: I'll shut up when you stop screwing up!

This inner battle always ended with Calder's pitches getting progressively wilder until he was pulled from the game. This is how we taught Calder to handle his inner critic:

Critic (after a ball or wild pitch): You suck!

Self listens but doesn't respond.

C: I'm talking to you. Control, man! Listen to me! You suck!

S: I'm listening. Do you have any suggestions?

C: Huh?

S: Do you have any helpful suggestions?

C: Don't overthrow!

S: Good suggestion. Thanks for your help.

C: That's it?

S: Yup!

Learning how to disengage from the struggle with the inner critic takes time, patience, *and a lot of practice.* In the beginning, it rarely goes as easily as depicted in the above dialogue. Perhaps the first step the athlete can take is to just *simply listen to the chatter from an outside "observer's stance" and not judge or evaluate what he or she hears. Do not fight with this part of the self;* just notice what it is saying. This observer stance will feel very different to the critic in you and will eventually take some of the steam out of its attack. When you respond to your inner critic as if it is an important part of your "team," it eventually begins to soften.

This ability to unemotionally track your mind from moment to moment without judgment is called "mindfulness," which comes from the practice of meditation. It is one of the mental skills that will ultimately help you to make the transition from performance block to performance expansion. In its essence, it is a way of learning to trust yourself, your deepest self.

In the next chapter we outline our pioneering treatment model for working with athletes. Based on the results that we have consistently obtained with all types of RSPPs across the wide range of sports, we believe that our treatment approach is groundbreaking and is destined to change the concepts and practices of the field of sports and performance psychology.

CHAPTER 9

TREATMENT
Brainspotting Sports Work in Action

Throughout this book, we have alluded to the treatment process. In this chapter, we provide a detailed outline of our unique approach. Based on the results that we have obtained, we believe our model is groundbreaking.

Dr. Goldberg working with junior golfer, Hannah Arnold

Traditional sports psychologists have missed the mark in working with slumps, blocks, anxiety, and RSPPs. Their approach, which I (AG) used for 17 years, addresses only *conscious symptoms*, rarely

150

reaching the underlying causes. By getting underneath to the causes such as past injuries and other traumas, we accomplish lasting, profound changes. We do this by utilizing powerful, focused tools that locate and release the traumas in the brain and body.

Brainspotting Sports Work has very little to do with traditional talk therapy. The belief in talk therapy is that talking about and reliving earlier upsets ultimately helps the client to heal. Talk therapy may uncover upsetting early childhood experiences that contribute to one's problems in the present, but the treatment is often lengthy and inefficient.

Talking doesn't reach sports trauma in the brain or body

Treatment that relies on *conscious verbal reporting* is problematic because the client often either is unable to articulate the problem or is unaware of it. Athletes struggling with RSPPs are unable to understand them because the freeze reactions have nothing to do with conscious processes but are instead products of traumas, often long forgotten, that are still unconsciously held in their bodies. The gymnast unable to go backward on the balance beam may be clueless of what she is experiencing before and during the skill. What she *is* aware of after mounting the beam is that she can't get her body to go backward. Talking to her about the problem and teaching her *conscious* strategies to overcome it are simply ineffective.

It was my (AG) repeated experiences of failure with many stuck athletes that convinced me that the more conscious cognitive sports psychology approach was inadequate in resolving RSPPs. The missing piece turned out to be the *athlete's body*, which always holds the clues to understanding and resolving the specific performance problem.

Brainspotting Sports Work explores past physical and emotional traumas without consciously rehashing them. As a consequence, we don't encourage athletes to talk or think through past events. Instead, our model directly targets the places in the athlete's brain and body where these physical and emotional traumas are frozen. Past experiences do emerge spontaneously in our process, and we have techniques to diminish and deactivate them—for instance, using Brainspotting, which uses eye position to locate where the brain is holding the problem. By holding the eye position in place, with the athlete gazing at a pointer, the brain is able to process and release the trauma's present-day effects. (We will describe and illustrate Brainspotting later in the chapter.) This healing tool helps athletes return to their "old selves," as the RSPP falls away when it has no legs to stand on.

As with other treatment models, ours starts with assessing the problem. An RSPP is a puzzle, and our attempt is to identify the intricate pieces necessary for a solution. How and when did the problem manifest itself? What is the athlete's physical experience of the problem? What emotions associate to the RSPP? How long has the RSPP been going on? When did it reach its worst point?

The athlete has been referred to us for a reason. Perhaps he is overwhelmed with preperformance anxiety and falls apart in important games or tryouts. Maybe she can no longer do backward tumbling because of an incapacitating fear of reinjury. Perhaps he shies away from hard contact and is tentative under pressure, or maybe she has been throwing up before games for six months. In clarifying the presenting problem, we pinpoint the circumstances of its onset. What was going on in the athlete's life when the RSPP first emerged? How did the athlete's coaches and parents respond? How are they responding now?

Most people in sports fail to realize that the emergence of an RSPP doesn't correspond to the *start* of the problem. Rather, all involved are witnessing the *end product* of a long sequence of accumulated events. The problem emerges with a "trigger event" such as an additional injury, poor performance, or an emotionally upsetting experience on or off the field.

A metaphor for this process is a tree falling. A tree doesn't suddenly uproot itself; it has been in the process of falling for a long time. During the preceding weeks, months, and years, the tree had been systematically weakened by numerous internal and external forces from disease, insect infestation, and climactic events. The final act of falling on a particularly stormy day is not a simple result of the powerful wind but of a long sequence of unseen forces.

Once we have a good idea of what the RSPP looks and feels like from the athlete's perspective, we explore its roots. As discussed in earlier chapters, our theory is that repetitive performance problems have a basis in trauma. Traumatic experiences are frozen in the athlete's brain and body, and this residue generates anxiety, fear, physical tightness, and tentativeness. By first identifying and then systematically processing each of these past traumas, the athlete is able to successfully overcome the RSPP and return to optimal performance.

We uncover the roots of the RSPP by taking extensive injury and trauma histories starting from as far back as the athlete can remember. We define "trauma" as anything that has been significantly physically or emotionally upsetting *to the individual.* This could be something that happened directly to the athlete or something the athlete witnessed happening to someone else. Coaches or parents may interpret the event as relatively benign, but *it's the athlete's experience that determines whether the event is traumatic or not.* A gymnast who gets spatially lost in the middle of a skill, lands on her back, and gets the wind knocked out of her might recall this event with terror. Despite the coach's dismissive comments that the fall was "routine," we include it in our trauma history because of its *emotional significance to the athlete.*

When we take an injury history, the athlete often claims that he or she has never *really* been injured or that it was "no big deal" and is now ancient history. This is especially true with male athletes who have a need to dismiss experiences of pain and injury as if they were a sign of weakness. *Just because an event has been consciously forgotten doesn't mean the body doesn't remember*, however. Seemingly minor injuries that are unconsciously stored in the athlete's nervous system can affect performance unless processed through.

Taking these histories is vital in Brainspotting Sports Work because it helps us to understand the roots of the problem and to individualize our treatment with each athlete. Sometimes this treatment

Diagram/Table #10
INJURY/TRAUMA HISTORY

Age 7	Mild concussion falling off bicycle
Age 9	Older brother in bad car accident – paralyzed as result
Age 10	Dislocated right elbow (throwing arm) when pushed backwards
Age 11	15 Stitches in right thumb from pushing hand through a window
	4 stitches in back of head banging into baseball backstop
	Got measles
Age 14	Broke left arm skiing
Age 15	Favorite coach leaves and moves cross country
	Cut from travel team
Age 17	Embarrassed by high school coach during State Tournament after striking out... college coaches watching
	Broke right thumb sliding into home
Age 18	Bad tendonitis in throwing arm for almost 4 months
Age 19	College coach benched me in big game after making errors
Age 20	Lost starting position to freshman
	Mom diagnosed with cancer

An injury history

process is straightforward; at other times, it is quite complex. James was referred to me (AG) because his skiing race times were much slower than those from the previous season. His coach told him he was sitting too far back on his skis and that he looked like he was skiing scared. Regardless of conscious technique changes, James was unable to get himself to lean forward and attack the course. His early history was

154

uneventful, and his only trauma had occurred during the previous season, when he had torn his right ACL on a fall while racing. We were able to process out the effects of this fall, and James quickly returned to top form.

Pam was a competitive cheerleader who was so worried before competitions that she literally made herself sick to her stomach. Her unintended preperformance ritual of throwing up drained her, sabotaged her performance, and jeopardized her starting position on the elite squad. Unlike James, Pam had an extensive injury history including two concussions, a broken wrist, a dislocated elbow, a dog bite to the face, and a fall out of a tree. This injury history was further complicated by an underlying anxiety disorder that worsened after her parents divorced when she was eight. The extensive nature of Pam's trauma history coupled with her anxiety disorder made the treatment process more complex and gradual than James', but with time and Brainspotting Sports Work, she was able to once again perform at a high level with no nausea or anxiety.

Depression complicates sports trauma

In the initial diagnostic work with a new client, we carefully sort out all personal and athletic factors, including relationships with coaches, parents, siblings, friends, and teammates. In our work, an underlying depression, like a preexisting anxiety condition, can complicate and lengthen treatment. Depression in an athlete is often "reactive" in response to his or her performance difficulties.

Serious athletes are usually high achievers and derive self-esteem through performing at the highest levels. They are known for their athletic accomplishments, which fuel their sense of specialness. When such athletes struggle, it's a blow to their identities and self-esteem. The pitcher noted for his speed, control, and athleticism who inexplicably can't find the strike zone faces a disturbing reality. What used to bring feelings of joy, pride, and accomplishment now leaves him with frustration, shame, and failure. The result of this "fall from grace" is depressive feelings that infiltrate his life.

The struggling elite athlete is plagued by intense anxiety in addition to depression. The anxiety manifests as obsessing about the problem and dread that "it" will recur. This anticipatory anxiety leaves the athlete in a state of internal danger that further tightens already tense muscles, distracts the focus, and ensures the persistence of the performance woes.

Performance anxiety is a byproduct of what we call the *magnifying glass effect*. Athletes often perform in front of audiences, which, depending on their competitive level, can run into the tens of thousands. The sports media overanalyzes athletes' performances, cruelly magnifying mistakes and failures. Public exposure generates intense humiliation and is traumatizing by itself. The overblown importance attached to sports outcome is a sure-fire formula for generating intense internal stress in athletes as their value as individuals is narrowly defined by how well they perform *today*. This practice creates a breeding ground for RSPPs.

Brainspotting Sports Work is based on a fundamental belief that every case is different and each treatment must be tailored to the specific needs of the athlete. Our treatment is always *exploratory* in nature. Accordingly, we don't have a preordained model that we fit each athlete into, as is done in traditional sports psychology. We don't teach athletes mental rehearsal, relaxation techniques, or methods for handling negative self-talk. Instead, we listen carefully to the unique story that each athlete's brain and body tell us about the origin and function of the performance problem. We allow each story to be our guide. This storytelling process guides the athlete to internally activate whatever bothers him or her.

Public exposure worsens sports traumas

As mentioned earlier in the chapter, the most essential of our tools is the technique developed by David Grand called Brainspotting. This is a comprehensive approach that powerfully finds the location of the trauma in the brain and the body remarkably by eye position. It is said that "the eyes are the window to the soul," but we have found that the eyes are also the window to the brain and the body. Dr. Grand discovered that eye location in a person that is activated around an issue reveals where the brain holds the trauma and where the body reflects it. And there are two ways of finding these specific eye positions.

In both ways we start by asking the client to shift his focus of attention internally and "activate" him or herself around the issue. Activation is the process of beginning to experience the anxiety provoking thoughts, emotions and body sensations. There are numerous ways to accomplish this activation. We might first ask the athlete to *mentally* put herself in the feared situation. The wild softball pitcher who is terrified of being hit by a ball coming back up the middle might vividly imagine it in the moment. Or we might *literally* take an

Diagram/Table #11
"SUDS" SCALE OR LEVEL OF ACTIVATION

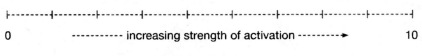

0 ---------- increasing strength of activation ---------➤ 10

The suds scale

athlete into their anxiety-provoking situation by taking a golfer who struggles with the chipping yips to a course and ask him to execute a 20–30 yard chip shot.

Next we have the athlete rate his or her level of activation from 0 to 10, where 0 reflects no activation and 10 represents the worst it can be. Numbers help us to see where we start, where we go in the process and when we are finished (when a 0 is attained). We "listen" carefully to what the body has to "tell" us by asking the athlete where he or she feels the activation in his or her body. When imagining throwing to an imposing batter, a struggling pitcher may notice a panicky feeling in his stomach and tightness in his throwing wrist. A golfer facing a chip may feel a tingling tension up and down her forearms and biceps. This physical tension can be accompanied by shame, which is experienced as heat in the face and neck. Once the location and intensity of the symptom activation has been determined, the athlete is then ready for the next step which is the key to Brainspotting.

We mentioned that there are two ways of finding the eye position that locates the problem in the brain and body. The first way is for the athlete to track the therapist's finger or a wand as it slowly moves across the visual field. The therapist closely observes the athlete's eyes and face, searching for reflexive responses. An example of this might be an eye wobble or freeze, a hard swallow, or a quick in-breath (countless other reflexes are also used). When any of these manifestations are observed, the therapist simply holds his or her finger still and asks the athlete to maintain the gaze. The activated trauma is now held and begins to unwind itself.

The second way to find the eye position again begins with having the athlete track the therapist's finger across his or her visual field, only this time, the therapist asks the athlete to notice in which eye position he or she feels the most activation in the body. Once they find the spot, they are ready to go, and the athlete gazes directly at the finger or pointer while they follow their internal experience moment to moment. In this way, the activated trauma is found and held in place as it begins to unwind itself.

As we track the activation in the athlete's body, the thoughts and movements that have knotted the athlete's performance begin to slowly unravel. The activation begins to release, and the athlete's distress level progressively diminishes. The processing part of the work that we do is not predictable or controllable; instead, it is a spontaneous expression in the moment of what's going on inside the athlete. The only assumption we make in our model is that the *answer lies within*.

The deep brain and body are far beyond the athlete's conscious awareness and are inaccessible to the thinking and speaking regions of the athlete's brain. The athlete's conscious mind will rarely understand and follow the connections that his deep brain makes during the activation and processing; however, **conscious understanding and insight are not necessary for the successful processing of accumulated trauma**. Let's look at Jerry for an example.

Jerry was a seasoned professional BMX racer who self-referred because of problems in his bigger races. He consistently rode relaxed and confidently in practice and in his less significant races. When it came to national-caliber events, however, he inexplicably became nervous and physically tight before races. His nervousness was fueled by negative self-talk about all the things that could go wrong during the race, including crashing and sustaining a serious injury. As a result of this anxiety, he rode defensively and slowly, far below his capabilities. Especially frustrating for Jerry was losing to much weaker riders. Three years prior, before this problem surfaced, Jerry had been one of the top riders in the country, winning numerous national and international events.

Jerry had sustained a number of traumas during his life and racing career. At 12, he broke a wrist on a fall from a horse. He suffered numerous concussions from crashes during races, accumulating four in just one year! Jerry also broke his thumb and his other wrist, and chipped a bone in his shoulder while racing. In a national race three years before his RSPP emerged, Jerry was riding when a racer behind him lost control and slammed into Jerry, propelling him over his handlebars. Jerry had landed on his shoulder, breaking it in three places. The injury was the most painful of his life and required surgery. He had not been the same since, feeling uncharacteristically timid when close to other riders bumping and jostling him.

Jerry was unknowingly suffering from classic symptoms of PTSD. His fear response to high-pressure races was a flashback to his trauma. This kind of fear-based, defensive reaction is also found in PTSD sufferers who have survived assaults, combat, industrial accidents, or motor vehicle collisions. A trauma therapist needs the know-how and the effective tools to be helpful to a trauma survivor. We have modified and expanded these tools from the trauma field to once and for all resolve the worst RSPPs.

Athletes suffer a unique form of PTSD

After taking an extensive injury history, I (AG) began the activation phase by having Jerry mentally replay this trigger event. The following dialogue, which took place while Jerry was *simultaneously listening to bilateral sounds*, which is integral to Brainspotting, highlights how the activation leads to the processing and resolution.

Dr. G: When you think about that particular crash, Jerry, what stands out the most for you now?

J: It looks and feels like it's happening *right now*. The pain is the worst part of it. It's excruciating and terrifying. It's the worst pain that I've ever felt in my life.

Dr. G: Can I assume that the pain is a 10 on that 0-to-10 scale?

J: It's a 20!

Dr. G: OK, now track this pointer with your eyes and let me know where you feel the most activation.

J (tracking right to left): Right there (pointing off to his left). I *really feel* it there.

Dr. G: OK, let's get right to work on it. Go inside and notice what comes next and then what follows that.

J (after 30 seconds): I'm laid out on the ground. The EMT is pushing and poking my shoulder, trying to move it, and I feel like taking his head off. He doesn't get that I'm in pain and he's making it worse. I feel like throwing up.

Dr. G: Keep going and see where it takes you.

J (after 30 seconds): This is weird. I'm seeing flipping picture images of the entire accident. They're going frame by frame. Now I'm in the hospital, nauseous as hell. I'm getting IV morphine. I feel the warmth running up my arm. Now everything's black. I'm out.

Dr. G: Keep looking at the pointer and see where it takes you.

J (after 45 seconds): Now I'm replaying some of the accidents with all those concussions. It's like I'm watching it on a screen, but I'm overwhelmed with anxiety. It's running around my body.

Dr. G: Good work. Keep going.

J (after 45 seconds): I'm seeing the original accident, but now it's in pieces. Other images are flipping through my head. The stress is down to a 5.

Dr. G: OK, let's see where that takes you.

J (after 30 seconds): This is really weird. The images are flashing and then breaking apart, and each time the anxiety drops a notch. It's down to a 3.

Dr. G: Great. Keep rolling.

J (after 30 seconds): I'm seeing random images from racing, but they're in black and white.

Dr. G: Keep going.

J (after 30 seconds): The film just replayed in fast forward. My body is down to a 1. And what's weird is my mind went completely blank.

Dr. G: Good stuff. Keep going.

J (after 45 seconds): My mind is still blank, and my body is very relaxed.

Dr. G: Good. Now let's check back to the very beginning. What does that accident look and feel like now when you bring it up?

J: Totally different. I can barely see it. This is weird. The pain is gone.

Dr. G: See where it goes from there.

J (after 30 seconds): That was strange. The whole thing replayed again in fast forward, only this time I didn't go over my handlebars. I just completed the race like it was normal. Then I jumped ahead to my next race. It feels like it almost didn't happen even though I can still remember it.

Dr. G: Great work, Jerry

J: How does this stuff work?

Dr. G: Your brain just healed itself, all by itself.

Jerry returned after his initial session and stated that for the first time in three years, he wasn't as nervous about his racing as he had been. In subsequent sessions, we processed his other traumas until he was unable to bring up any physical or emotional distress when he thought about them. Some were on the same Brainspot off to the left, whereas others were in different eye locations.

Two weeks after this session he competed in a regional race and reported that he had been banging elbows with other riders and hadn't backed off. In fact, *he hadn't even been aware* of the contact until his wife later pointed out that he looked like his old, confident self. He then realized that his fear hadn't been triggered during the jostling. What's clear from Jerry's case and the dialogue from his session is how neurological the treatment process with RSPPs is. The amazing imagery that Jerry reported was his brain spontaneously healing itself moment by moment. I did not lead him through any specific set of directions. Once he was activated and focused on a Brainspot, I trusted his brain to know exactly where to go. I simply followed along.

The processing, which is integral to our work, follows the principle that the answer lies within. The athlete's deep brain knows exactly where to go to find and release the problem. Once an issue has been activated in the athlete's brain and body, the processing works by having the athlete adopt a "let-it-happen" observer's stance. The individual is instructed to follow his or her internal experience wherever it leads, step-by-step. The athlete is guided to let go of all expectations and judgments and to not consciously try to guide the process other than maintaining a stance of relaxed curiosity as he or she watches the mind jump around. This relaxed, nonjudgmental, let-it-happen stance parallels the mindset an athlete needs to adopt for optimal performance. In fact, when athletes talk about being "in the zone," that elusive state of expanded performance, they describe the same kind of easy, let-it-happen mindset.

As illustrated in Jerry's case, some traumas process quickly. With other traumas, the processing may need more time. Throughout the processing, we listen carefully to the athlete's body to hear echoes of past injuries and traumas.

Micro-movement finds and releases traumas in the body

Another important way we listen to the athlete's brain and body is a technique that we call **micro-movement**. Micro-movement involves having the athlete physically go through the actual movements that he or she struggles with, but in extreme slow motion. We have the golfer swing, the pitcher throw, the soccer keeper dive to his right, the batter take a cut, or the gymnast start a back walkover in extreme slow motion.

As the athlete goes through these motions, we look for minute signs of physical or emotional tension, such as jerks, jumps, or twitches, that disrupt the smooth execution and fluidity of the movement. We also ask the athlete to report any internal physical or emotional distress that may arise in this process. When we locate a spot where the movement is disrupted, we guide the athlete to hold the position and observe what comes up. This is continued, step-by-step, through the movement. These jumps and jerks indicate where negative experiences have been stored in the body. Our micro-movement technique helps find and release the experiences. This technique promotes enhanced fluidity and confidence by releasing silently accumulated experiences held throughout the movement.

A variation of micro-movement guides the athlete to physically reenact an injury in extreme slow motion. The ski racer who blew out his ACL was encouraged to gradually replay the actual movements where he caught the edge, lost control, and then began to fall. The gymnast who broke her arm was instructed to replay the impact of falling backward in slow motion. For the pitcher struck in the head by a hard line drive up the middle, we held a ball ten feet from him and moved it toward him extremely slowly. As with all micro-movement exercises, we closely monitor the athlete's physical and emotional responses. Whenever the distress level or physical sensations arise, we guide the individual to freeze in that position and observe his or her internal process. This helps to both release and complete the interrupted experience.

It's important to note that one can't activate the body without simultaneously activating the brain. Everything that is felt in the body is mirrored in the brain. Micro-movement identifies and releases dually held injuries and traumas. The brain observes itself and locates and focuses on the problem in the body.

We trust that the athlete's brain and body hold the answer, and accordingly, our treatment *follows* athletes rather than *leads* them, which is what is done in most sports-psychology approaches. In most methods, the sports psychologist is assumed to have the answers and therefore directly provides these answers and teaches techniques to the athlete. If performance doesn't improve, it's the sports psychologist's job to try something else to fix the problem. In this way, the traditional sports psychology model for RSPPs both *directs* and *prescribes* solutions.

In our model, we *collaborate with* the athlete in the same way a pitcher and catcher work together. The client-athlete is the pitcher who *initiates* the action, and we, the therapists, are the catchers who *receive* the action. Although the catcher calls the signals, it's the pitcher's job to receive them and decide whether to go with them. In this way, the pitcher ultimately does most of the work and the catcher has minimal control over the pitches.

As we've mentioned before, we bilaterally stimulate the brain to drive the processing. This is accomplished by having the athlete listen

The conscious brain receives the wisdom of the deeper brain

to a specially designed CD that directs sound to flow continuously between the left and right ears. The other primary tool is Brainspotting, which we discussed earlier. Here is an exercise that demonstrates how the initial stages of the activation and processing work:

Step 1—Remember an embarrassing performance or upsetting sports injury.

Step 2—As you replay the incident, notice what's going on in your body. Be aware of how quickly your body registers and expresses this negative experience. Don't try to control what is happening. Simply *observe where your mind goes and the physical feelings and emotions that may arise.* If emotions arise, notice *where you feel them in your body.* If you become aware of any *physical sensations* like muscle tension or pain, *notice their location in your body.* Rate the strength of these physical and emotional responses on a scale of 0 to 10, where 0 represents no response and 10 represents the most intense response.

Step 3—With your eyes closed, let your mind go anywhere for 60 seconds. Notice what comes next and then what follows.

Step 4—Now check the sensations that you started with in your body. Where are they now?

Step 5—Once again, allow your mind to go anywhere for an additional minute or two.

Step 6—Now check again on the feelings of discomfort. Where are they now in your body? Rate them once again on the 0-to-10 scale.

Step 7—Allow your self-observance to travel for another minute or so.

Step 8—Return to the original upsetting experience. What, if anything, has changed about it mentally, physically, or emotionally? Is the picture brighter and more detailed? Does it appear faded or more distant? Are the emotions stronger, weaker, or unchanged? Have the physical sensations in your body changed or remained the same? Once more, rate the intensity of your physical sensations on the 0-to-10 scale and check out where you are holding them in your body.

In this brief exercise, you can begin to get a sense of the work, although without the power of the bilateral sound. Of course, actual ongoing treatment with Brainspotting Sports Work is far more focused and powerful than this introductory experience.

We'd also like to give you an additional taste of Brainspotting. Start with Steps 1 and 2 outlined above, then move to Step 3 here:

Step 3—Look to your left and chose an object to focus on. Gaze at the object for 10 seconds. Next, bring your eyes to the middle and focus on an object straight ahead for 10 seconds. Now shift your eyes to the right and find an object to focus on and gaze at it for 10 seconds. Notice which of these three directions produces the highest level of activation, or the strongest physical sensations.

Step 4—Move your gaze to the object either left, center, or right, where the activation was the highest and gaze at it for 60 seconds. Observe the flow of your inner experience—thoughts, emotions, body sensations, and memories—as it arises and passes. As you continue to gaze at the same spot, follow the directions in Steps 4 through 8 as outlined above.

By determining these relevant eye positions and then assessing numerically (0–10) the intensity of your subsequent responses, you actually determine the location of the frozen negative experience in your brain and body. When you maintain this eye position as you follow your drifting mind, your brain processes and releases deeply and thoroughly whatever is blocking or bothering you.

This chapter has outlined how Brainspotting Sports Work offers breakthroughs for resolving RSPPs that far exceed the cognitive-behavioral strategies used by most sports psychologists. This is critical for resolving repetitive performance difficulties because these problems can't be eliminated without getting to the root of the problem. The physical tightness, self-doubts, and negative thinking so common to

RSPPs are simply the surface symptoms of the problem. When sports psychology is confined to treating symptoms without focusing on the underlying source, the results achieved are consistently limited. If the athlete does happen to experience improvement with the repetitive problem in such treatment, the relief usually is short lasting.

In Chapter 10, we discuss self-help strategies that address RSPPs. Although fully resolving trauma-based performance problems usually requires the guidance of a trained professional, we present exercises that help to get the process rolling.

CHAPTER 10

SELF-HELP FOR REPETITIVE SPORTS PERFORMANCE PROBLEMS
WHAT YOU CAN DO TO GET YOURSELF UNSTUCK AND BACK
ON TRACK

Serious athletes rely on steely wills and old-fashioned hard work to master problems and overcome obstacles. RSPPs leave them feeling powerless to change their situations. Attacking a problem with hard work is most often responsible for the athlete's accomplishments, and "trying harder" is their most effective tried-and-true success strategy.

When athletes suddenly can't make a simple throw or perform at their usual high levels, however, they discover that their strategy of working harder *doesn't work*. Most athletes who approach their performance problems with extra effort soon discover that their performance actually *worsens*. "Trying harder" tightens athletes up mentally and physically, making smooth, well-timed execution impossible, so these athletes continue to struggle and fail, and their frustration levels rise.

It's as if the key that would unlock the difficulty is jammed in the lock. The athlete becomes frustrated with the stuckness and forces the key in a futile attempt to free it. What the athlete doesn't realize is that when he or she continues to use force, the mechanism becomes more jammed; if the athlete continues to pressure the lock, the key eventually snaps off. The athlete is unaware that a gentler, more relaxed approach to the problem is required.

Because athletes need to be mentally and physically relaxed to perform at their potential, frustration and self-directed anger trigger downward spirals. Soon, they battle feelings that they may never be able to turn things around. The failure of the trying-harder strategy leaves them feeling confused and powerless. These feelings of confusion and powerlessness are what we directly address in this chapter. Is it possible to break free from the clutches of a repetitive performance problem by yourself?

It's important to understand that on your own, you can't replicate the precise, powerful work of being guided by an expert trained in Brainspotting Sports Work. There are still many things you can do using our techniques, however. When consistently and properly used by themselves, these exercises and strategies are quite powerful and effective.

#1—TAKING YOUR OWN SPORTS INJURY AND TRAUMA HISTORY

As we've discussed throughout this book, RSPPs have underlying trauma bases. One of the first steps in resolving an RSPP is discovering what physical or emotional traumas are unknowingly fueling your fears and blocks. *In taking your sports trauma history, keep in mind that your belief that a past incident was "no big deal" or couldn't possibly be related to your current problem is usually inaccurate.* Your conscious mind, left to its own devices, can't comprehend how the brain-body system works, so as you compile this history, suspend your judgment and include *every* incident that comes to mind that involved *any* physical and/or emotional upsets.

Keep in mind that "trauma" means any event that *you* experienced as hurtful or upsetting at the time. Physical traumas are bad falls, collisions, sprained ankles, pulled muscles, broken bones, and near misses. You don't have to actually get hurt for an experience to be traumatic to you. Seeing someone else get badly injured can have a *big* traumatic effect on people. Emotional traumas can include costing your team a championship, making an error that results in a tough loss, or having to deal with a coach who is consistently angry, critical, and emotionally abusive.

As you compile your trauma history, be sure to include experiences both in and out of the athletic arena. Experiences from outside the arena may include falling out of trees, crashing your bicycle, wiping out on a skateboard, any kind of face-plant, surviving a bad car accident, having to

Witnessing a sports trauma can be traumatizing

move and saying goodbye to your close friends, watching your parents fight, experiencing your parents' divorce, or experiencing the death of a grandparent, close friend, family member, or beloved pet. Any trips to the hospital emergency room or surgical procedures should also be included in the history. Keep in mind that surgery under general anesthesia is registered as a trauma to the body.

Arrange your history in chronological order as best you can, and be sure to note anything that still elicits an emotional and/or physical charge. That is, as you remember a particular experience, you might find yourself instinctively shivering, grimacing, or responding with fear as if the incident just happened. Any past experience that elicits this kind of physical and emotional charge in the present is important in unraveling the mystery of your performance problem.

Once you've completed this list, try the following steps:

Step 1—Close your eyes and think about your current performance problem. Notice the associated feelings and *where you feel them right now in your body*. Allow yourself to see, hear, and feel the experience in the present.

172

Step 2—Keep your eyes closed and ask yourself, "What memory has to do with this?" *Without consciously or deliberately trying to think of an answer to this question,* notice the first thing that pops into your head. Even if the answer seems initially unrelated, *do not* dismiss it. Very often, your deeper brain will make the right connections by itself. The memory that does pop up may very well have something important to do with your performance woes. Flag it for future exercises in this chapter, then simply allow your mind to relax and go anywhere it chooses. Follow your train of thought as long as it is moving. Do not judge or dismiss anything that comes up.

#2—BILATERAL STIMULATION AND EYE POSITION

In Chapter 9, we discussed bilateral stimulation and eye position as the mechanisms that drive the processing in Brainspotting Sports Work. Bilateral stimulation represents the alternating, back-and-forth activation of the right and left hemispheres of the brain and is accomplished by listening to sounds traveling back and forth from the left ear to the right, physical touch going from the left side of the body to the right, or having one's eyes scan back and forth horizontally.

Eye position, which comes from Dr. Grand's discovery of Brainspotting, helps reveal where you're holding the negative experience in the brain. As you look between left, right, and center, you will notice your distress rise and fall when you're thinking about the sports trauma. If you stop at the exact spot where the intensity is greatest, you have found where the experience is held in your brain. When you notice where you're holding it in your body and just watch where your mind wanders on its own, the trauma begins to unwind. If you stay with it long enough, it will reduce and possibly go away.

When you combine this relevant eye position with bilateral stimulation, you have harnessed a powerhouse of focused healing. Our preferred tool to use for the left-right activation is the BioLateral audio CD produced by Dr. Grand. The CD combines calming sound movement with specially developed healing music and nature sounds. In addition to sound, we occasionally use back-and-forth eye movement to drive the processing. For the exercises in this chapter, we recommend that you use either the BioLateral CD or touch bilateral stimulation. To accomplish this, lightly squeeze your fists, alternating between your left and right (you may also do this by squeezing your thumb and forefinger).

When you use bilateral stimulation without focused activation—that is, without specifically thinking of something upsetting—the result is a relaxation response. At first your brain explores whatever is on your mind, consciously or unconsciously, and then it slows down into a more meditative, Zen-like state with body relaxation.

Bilateral stimulation of the brain combined with the images, sounds, emotions, and physical sensations from the remembered trauma is then focused when you find the eye position (left, center, or right) that feels the most active. Following the processing helps unwind the upsetting experience until it's lost its emotional hold on you.

Both of the following two exercises, as well as all of the other self-help strategies in this chapter, involve the use of *mindfulness*. Mindfulness is a form of self-observation found in any meditation practice in which you allow the focus of your concentration to gently follow your thoughts, physical feelings, and emotions as they change, moment by moment, in the present.

If you've used meditation or any mindfulness or awareness exercises before, you're already familiar with this process. When you combine mindfulness with bilateral stimulation and eye position, you'll find the experience more powerful and focused (that's why we call it focused mindfulness). If you're not familiar with meditation or mindfulness, you will still find it easy to do.

#2A—USING LEFT-RIGHT TACTILE STIMULATION

The most common form of tactile bilateral stimulation is alternating the gentle squeezing of your left and right fists. If you choose this method, be sure that the squeezing is done very lightly. Walking is

Brainspotting Sports Work healing uses mindfulness

another form of bilateral stimulation because as you step, you naturally alternate the movement of the left and the right sides of your body. In fact, this is a way that human beings have been processing information for ages—it's the old, "I think I'll take a walk and think that over."

Step 1—Sit or lie comfortably in a place where you will be undisturbed for 10 minutes or more. Close your eyes and begin to slowly alternate gently squeezing your fists left and right. Allow your mind to drift, and notice what's on your mind, how you're feeling emotionally and in your body. It's like sitting in the passenger seat, gazing out the window, just noticing what passes by. Just notice what comes next, then what comes after that. Don't be concerned if things that come up seem unrelated or confusing. You are simply watching your deeper brain in action. Continue the squeezing for a minute or two.

Step 2—Check in to see what you are feeling, and where you're feeling it in your body. Continue the gentle squeezing for another one to two minutes, and as your mind jumps around, notice where it goes and what comes up. Periodically check in with how you're feeling in your body.

Step 3—After a few minutes, you may notice feelings of relaxation in your body, like a comfortable heaviness in your arms or legs or a sensation of tingling in your fingers and hands. As these feelings arise, simply notice their location and follow them as they move around your body. You may also become aware that your mind quiets and even goes blank. This is an indication that you have achieved a relaxed, balanced state. Continue the back-and-forth squeezing for 5 or 10 minutes, noticing the relaxation in your body. At the end of the exercise, notice how you feel. After you've tried this exercise once or twice, you are ready for more focused work.

#2B—WORKING ON A NEGATIVE PERFORMANCE EXPERIENCE USING EYE POSITION

Brainspotting in action

176

Step 1—Sit or lie comfortably in a place where you will be undisturbed for 10 minutes or more. Think about a sports situation past or present that's still bothering you. You may even begin to feel your body moving as if you were in the original experience. Rate the intensity of how much it is bothering you, from 0, which means not at all, to 10, which is the most it can be. Then see where you are holding the upset feeling in your body. Now we're going to find the eye position that holds the core of the experience. Look at an object to your right and stare at it for 10 seconds. Then stare straight ahead at another object for another 10 seconds. Then choose an object to your left and repeat the procedure. Either to your right, straight ahead or to your left, notice where the experience feels the most intense or bothersome. Whichever it is, stare at that one spot and notice how you feel in your body.

Step 2—Allow your mind to drift, noticing what's on your mind, how you're feeling emotionally and in your body. Just notice what comes next, then what comes after that. Don't be concerned if things that come up seem unrelated or confusing. A kind of quick jumping around reflects that your brain is working actively even if you can't understand it. Just sit back and observe whatever comes up. Let your mind go freely in any direction that it wants. As you do so, notice what you feel in your body and where you feel it.

Step 3—After two to three minutes, check back to your original starting point. Notice what the image looks like now, the emotions that come with it, and, most important, how you feel in your body. From your awareness of the body sensations, allow your mind to go for an additional two to three minutes.

Step 4—Continue to do *several* more of these short processing "sets," and after each one, check back to the original experience to see where it is now in terms of clarity, detail and intensity. As you proceed with this exercise, you may notice that your original experience begins to look and feel different. Perhaps it seems faded or even further away. These changes show that the experience is being stored more deeply in your memory banks and that the process is working. In fact, after some processing, you may not be able to bring up the original image at all.

We often utilize Brainspotting in our work with athletes, sometimes by itself and frequently in conjunction with auditory stimulation. Whether done in session or used for self-help, the combination of the two techniques is the real powerhouse of performance change. After experimenting with this procedure, you'll probably be ready to use these tools to focus directly on a specific performance block that you are currently struggling with or on a more upsetting sports trauma.

#3—WORKING WITH A CURRENT PERFORMANCE BLOCK OR SIGNIFICANT SPORTS TRAUMA

Self-work can release sports trauma

Step 1—Select a sports performance problem that you are presently struggling with or a past injury or trauma that is emotionally active for you. Remember that this trauma can be physical and/or emotional. Your selection can be of a recent event or one that is from your past. For this exercise, it's best to pick a target that brings up a *strong reaction* within you. A good choice would be something that you're afraid will happen again, like making a big mistake at a crucial time, choking, getting humiliated by your coach, or getting reinjured. Don't be afraid to choose a target that brings up strong feelings. The more powerful the emotion, the more you'll release through the processing.

Step 2—Once you've selected your target, close your eyes and mentally bring yourself back to the experience, taking all the time you need to let it arise within you. You can make this a sensory process by noticing in detail all that you see, hear, feel, and/or smell. Notice also what, if any, emotions are attached to this experience. Very often, these events can be quite powerful and may trigger feelings of fear, confusion, anger, sadness, or embarrassment. Using the 0–10 rating scale, choose the number that represents the intensity of what you are experiencing. Remember, 0 represents no distress and 10 represents the worst distress possible. Don't get hung up on the accuracy of the number, because it is subjective. Next, focus on exactly where in your body you are holding this distress.

Step 3—Now find the eye position that holds the core of this experience. Look at an object to your right and stare at it for 10 seconds. Then stare straight ahead at another object for another 10 seconds. Then choose an object to your left and repeat the procedure. Either to your right, straight ahead, or to your left, notice where the experience feels the most intense or bothersome. Whichever it is, stare at that one spot and notice how you feel in your body. Then begin your bilateral stimulation (fist squeezing) and remember to continue it for the entire exercise.

Step 4—Allow your mind to travel on its own for one to two minutes, noticing what comes up. Remember to keep an objective observer's stance throughout this exercise. You don't want to evaluate what comes up or consciously direct your thinking. After a minute or so, check in with how you're feeling and where you're feeling it in your body.

Step 5—Proceed with two or three of these one- to two-minute "sets," checking in with yourself after each one to see what you're feeling and where you're holding the experience in your body. Once you've done a few of these shorter sets, do several longer ones, checking in every three to five minutes.

Step 6—When you think the original incident has lost most of its emotional punch, go back and check in on it. When you do, once again notice what you see, hear, feel, and smell. What do you feel in your body, and where do you feel it? Again, use the 0–10 scale to measure the strength of the distress that may be left. If the distress is a 2 or lower, do a few more sets until you can no longer activate any distress with the original experience. If the distress is a 3 or higher, go back to Step 4 and continue to process for as many sets as necessary. At the end of these sets, check back to the original experience and see where it's at.

When you return to the original incident and can't generate any distress, you can finish the exercise or go for a few more sets to deepen your relaxation and expansion. Remember that this is a powerful process so you may feel tired or a little "out of it" when you finish. This is actually a good sign because it shows that your brain has done the "heavy lifting," freeing you from the grips of the sports trauma. Accordingly, *it's important to not do this exercise right before practice or a competition;* instead, try it out when you have free time that's not close to a performance.

It's also essential to keep in mind that just one trial of this exercise is usually not enough to fully release you from what is holding you back. In fact, after one or two times, you may still notice that your distress level remains above a 3 as you approach a performance. If this is the case, continue to use the exercise until you can better contain the distress. A day or two after your first self-session, go out into your performance arena and observe any changes in your mental or physical responses. These differences may be small, involving minor attitude changes, less fear, or slight increase in relaxation. You may, however, notice more significant and obvious positive changes. Don't be alarmed if you observe an increase in negative thoughts or anxiety. Whatever differences you notice, we encourage you to trust the process and bring it back with you to your next self-session.

If the changes that you noticed were positive, start by focusing on them in your next self-session. If the changes were negative or reflected an increase in distress, begin with these feelings. You can also start your next session by directly focusing on any remaining block, fear, or doubts.

Try to avoid placing expectations on your self-sessions to immediately and dramatically remove your fears or eliminate your performance problem. It's these same expectations that are feeding your performance difficulties. Performance expectations will interfere with the process of the exercises and keep you stuck. (For a more in-depth discussion of the destructive power of performance expectations, see Chapter 7.)

This can be a challenge, because you are reading this book and working with these exercises to release your performance problems. How can you *not* have expectations of getting unstuck and returning to form? Simply put, when you walk onto the field, court, floor, or course, you want to perform well and win. Expanded performance and winning usually happen when we are not focused on the *outcome* but instead on the *process* of the performance. The same holds true in your self-sessions. Positive changes find their own way, not the path of anticipation or expectation. Be open to any change, regardless of how small, and be ready and watchful for surprises.

#4—INJURY RECOVERY AND FEAR OF REINJURY

The techniques of Brainspotting Sports Work are also effective with both injury recovery and the fear of reinjury. All athletes experience physical traumas during their careers. Some athletes have fewer or less-extensive injuries. Others sustain multiple, more serious injuries, some of which require surgery and extensive rehab. As we've discussed throughout the book, injuries are not traumas only to the body but also to the mind.

When an injury has healed and you're cleared by your doctor to play, your mind might not be as ready and willing to return as your body is. It is normal to feel "gun shy" and that you will get hurt again if you go all-out. Regardless of how powerful these feelings are, know that they are normal and inescapable. We tend to experience these worries in our "anxiety spots" such as the head, throat, chest, stomach, and back, as well as in the physical location of the injury itself, for example the knee, shoulder, elbow, or ankle.

You can use the following exercise while recovering from an injury or when returning post-injury:

Part 1—Injury Recovery

Step 1—Find a quiet space where you will be undisturbed for 15–20 minutes. Close your eyes and bring up the memory of your injury and how it occurred. Notice what you see, hear, feel, or smell. Be aware of any emotions that are attached to this experience and where you feel them in your body. Using the 0–10 rating scale to measure the strength of your *current feelings*, let a number pop into your mind. Pay particularly close attention to the area in your body that was hurt.

Step 2—Find the eye position that holds the core of the injury experience. Look at an object to your right and stare at it for 10 seconds. Then stare straight ahead at another object for another 10 seconds. Then choose an object to your left and repeat the procedure. Either to your right, straight ahead, or to your left, notice where the injury experience feels the most intense. Wherever it is, stare at that one spot and again notice how you feel in your body. Next, begin your bilateral stimulation (fist squeezing) and remember to continue it for the entire exercise.

Step 3—Maintaining this eye position, allow your mind to replay the injury in any way that it wants to. You may find that your mind runs through the event from start to finish or that it instead jumps around. You may also notice that as your mind does this, it may jump to other related or unrelated injuries. Don't try to consciously direct or censor what comes up. Just notice where your mind goes and what you see, hear, and feel in your body. Do this for a two- to three-minute set.

Step 4—Check back to see what you are feeling and where you are feeling it in your body. Keeping this same eye position, do several more of these two- to three-minute sets. Check back with yourself after each one and note the intensity and location of your physical sensations and what is going on with the internal images. Once you've done a few of these shorter sets, do several longer ones of four to five minutes.

Step 5—Bring up the original injury and again notice what you see, hear, and feel. Be aware of any physical sensations in your body and especially around the injury site. Again, use the 0–10 rating system to measure the strength of the distress that remains. If the distress is a 2 or lower, do a few more sets until you can't activate any distress from the injury. If the distress is a 3 or higher, return to Step 2 and continue to process until the distress is released.

When the distress is a 0 as you think of the injury, you're ready to proceed to the second part of this exercise. Remember that this is powerful work and you may feel tired and a little "out of it" when you finish; therefore, be sure to not do this kind of work *right before practice or competitions.*

As in the previous exercise, it may take a number of times before you're able to completely release the injury-related physical and emotional feelings. If you don't notice much of a difference, be patient with yourself and keep going.

Part 2—Overcoming the Fear of Re-Injury

Self-work can release the fear of re-injury

Step 1—If you are continuing from Part 1, "Injury Recovery," maintain the same eye position in Part 2 and close your eyes and anticipate returning to game play. Be aware of any fears and negative thoughts that still remain related to re-injury. Don't be afraid to crank these fears up, as the more distress you generate, the more you'll release in the end. Notice any negative images, thoughts, emotions, or body sensations. Rate the intensity of your distress from 0 to 10.

If you're not continuing from Part 1, "Injury Recovery," find the Brainspot that's related to your fear of reinjury. Look at an object to your right and stare at it for 10 seconds. Then stare straight ahead at another object for another 10 seconds. Then choose an object to your left and repeat the procedure. Either to your right, straight ahead, or to your left, notice where the injury experience feels the most intense. Keep looking at that spot as you proceed.

Step 2—Using bilateral stimulation, allow your mind to explore on its own for a two- to three-minute set. If you begin to imagine yourself getting hurt again, don't interrupt this imagery, because if given a chance, it will play itself out. At the end of the set, try to experience your anticipated return to play and see how you experience it now.

Step 3—Continue with several more two- to three-minute sets, allowing your mind to go wherever it wants. Once you've done a few of these shorter sets, do several longer ones, again noticing how you're doing after every three to five minutes, checking in especially with what you're feeling in your body.

Step 4—Once again, imagine returning to your sport and check on your fears and negative thinking. Notice what you're feeling and where you're feeling it in your body. Rate any remaining distress from 0 to 10. Process out any remaining distress by doing as many three- to five-minute sets as needed to get your discomfort down to a 0.

Step 5—When you are no longer able to feel any distress about returning to your sport, deliberately bring up the "what ifs" (What if IT happens again? What if I'm not as good? What if I've been replaced?). Push your anxiety up as high as possible by imagining your worst fears coming true. Then let your mind process for three to five minutes and notice what comes up. If any distress still remains, continue to process in these three- to five-minute sets until you are unable to bring up any discomfort when you think about the "what ifs."

Step 6—Now that you've released your fears about returning, it's time to shift to the positive. While maintaining the same Brainspot, think back to how you played before your injury. Notice what you see and feel when you recall playing at your best. Your brain and body hold these muscle memories, and with the negative cleared away, the memories are easy to reactivate. It can help the process if you actually feel your body throwing the ball, taking a swing, or sticking a dismount. Spend one or more two- to three-minute sets reviewing some of these preinjury, peak performances.

Step 7—With the awareness of these good feelings, allow yourself to project into the future. In as much detail as possible, imagine yourself performing the way that you used to. See, hear, and feel yourself executing the way that you'd like, feeling relaxed and comfortable. Spend several two- to three-minute sets "practicing" experiencing these good feelings.

Self-work can lead to performance expansion

#6—PERFORMANCE TECHNIQUES TO BE USED JUST PRIOR TO OR DURING COMPETITION

Self-work can be done right before a competition

The following strategies can be used *right before* a game, match, or race and even, depending on whether your sport has natural breaks in the action, *during* those breaks. Such a break can be just a few seconds or as long as half time.

A) <u>Stretching with awareness and bilateral stimulation</u> (preperformance): As we've previously discussed, stretching with awareness is an effective method for getting physically and mentally relaxed before competition. Stretching with awareness means that *as* you stretch,

you maintain the focus of your concentration on the muscle group you are stretching. Focusing on the feeling of the stretch within your body distracts your conscious mind from thoughts that generate anxiety and tension, like your opponents, the outcome of the competition, a past bad performance, or the "what ifs." Combining this kind of stretching with bilateral squeezing heightens the physical and mental relaxation effect.

Step 1—Gently move your eyes left to right, either with eyes open or closed. *Be sure to continue this gentle movement for the entire exercise.* Shift your attention to the first muscle

Bilateral stimulation enhances stretching

group that you usually stretch. As you begin to feel the stretch in those muscles, focus on your breathing and inhale slowly into the stretch and then exhale slowly. Hold the tension for 20 seconds, continuing to breathe comfortably and slowly. Repeat the entire process with the same muscle group.

Step 2—Continue the process in Step 1 with each muscle group that you typically stretch before a performance.

B) <u>Maintaining composure during breaks in performance utilizing the bilateral fist-squeeze technique</u>: If your sport has regular, natural breaks in the flow of the performance like baseball, golf, basketball, ice hockey, tennis, softball, and football, you can use these intervals to help keep yourself calm and composed. For example, when you are upset by a mistake, a bad call, or a negative comment from your coach, you can take a few seconds of bilateral fist-squeezing to center and calm yourself.

With your eyes open or closed, alternate the gentle squeezing between your right and left fists. This can be done while you're on the bench, out in the field between plays, or during timeouts. As thoughts and emotions emerge, notice these without judging or trying to interfere with them. Continue for several seconds before the action restarts, and then refocus your concentration on the task at hand. Regular use of this bilateral stimulation will help you let go of the upset and mentally return to action.

C) <u>Centering through your breathing</u>: Awareness of your breathing helps center and ground you. An easy way to do this is by simply "listening" to your inhalation and exhalation without consciously trying to control your breathing in any way. You may initially notice your breath is fast and shallow or slower and deeper. Regardless, just follow your breath in and out. You can do this with or without the use of the bilateral fist squeezing. This simple act of noticing your breathing will ultimately calm you down and keep you in the "now" as the wisdom of your brain and body take over.

At a break in the action, gently shift your awareness to your diaphragm and follow your breath in and out. Notice the depth and speed of your breathing, but do not do anything to consciously change it. You can use this technique with your eyes either open or closed. Just before play resumes, allow your focus to return to the task at hand.

D) <u>Deepening an expanded performance feeling</u>: There is a specific physical and emotional feel that goes with expanded performance. By mentally replaying this feeling and combining your mental rehearsal with eye position and bilateral stimulation, you can increase the chances that your next performance will mirror these past great performances. Use this exercise the night before or the day of a performance.

Step 1—Close your eyes and think back to your most recent or any memorable great performance. Allow your mind to review the sights, sounds, and feelings of this experience, focusing on what you felt in your body as the performance unfolded. These "expanded performance feelings"

Brainspotting Sports Work helps athletes who are at their best to further expand their performance

have been automatically memorized and stored in your brain and body and can be tapped into for future use.

Step 2—Find the Brainspot that goes with this *positive* experience. Look at an object to your right and stare at it for 10 seconds. Then stare straight ahead at another object for 10 seconds. Next, choose an object to your left and repeat the same procedure. Either to your right, straight ahead, or to your left, notice where you feel the best or most connected to your great performance. Keep looking at that spot as you proceed, as it will help you to lock in and deepen those good feelings.

Step 3—Alternate the gentle squeezing between your right and left fists with the awareness of the good feelings and where you hold them in your body. Allow your mind to explore on its own for one to two minutes. You may notice that you begin to remember other good performances. Watch what comes up and keep an awareness of what you feel in your body.

Step 4—On the positive Brainspot, check back to those good feelings. They may have gotten stronger, gotten weaker, or moved around in your body. Again, just notice what you feel and let your mind go for another one- to two-minute set.

Step 5—After checking back to where those good feelings are at now, project ahead to an upcoming performance. With the awareness of the good feelings in your mind and body, let your mind preview this future performance in any way it would like.

Step 6—Do several more sets in which you go back and forth between the past great performance and the anticipated future one. Let it flow back and forth as you maintain awareness of the feelings that come up and where you feel them in your body.

We have presented you with a variety of exercises in this chapter to give you a feel of how we work and to give you some tools to address your RSPP on your own. You may find one or more of these exercises helpful in easing or even eliminating your RSPP. Remember that these kinds of performance problems are complicated and often require the help of a trained practitioner of Brainspotting Sports Work to uncover the roots and process through any underlying sports traumas, but if you find these self-help exercises useful, we encourage you to continue them as well as experimenting with the other techniques.

Try to remember that what you most need in your battle against any RSPP is patience. It is also critical that you be kind to yourself throughout the process. Impatience and self-directed anger only make you more stuck and further undermine your self-confidence. Instead, you need to be a supportive "good coach" to yourself, which creates an internal atmosphere of safety critical to the resolution of any RSPP.

CONCLUSION

Physically and emotionally upsetting events, or what we've been calling trauma throughout this book, are a natural part of the human condition. You can't go through life without experiencing numerous events that have a traumatic effect on you. When you participate in competitive sports, the likelihood of encountering these kinds of upsets increases. Whether we were humiliated, frightened, or injured, these traumas have a significant, and often hidden, impact on our performances and on our psychological well-being.

Sports is a concentrated version of our daily lives. Performances are time-limited, played in an enclosed area, and have high stakes attached to the outcome, so there's a greater opportunity for traumatic exposure with lasting consequences for people as individuals and athletes. *It is the gradual, unconscious accumulation of these upsetting experiences in the brain and body, tracing back to childhood sports, that we have discovered as the primary cause of repetitive performance problems like performance anxiety, blocks, and the yips.*

Traditional methods for dealing with these recurring problems have focused on the *surface* of the problem. These include the athlete's symptoms of anxiety, obsessive self-doubt and negative thinking, physical tension, and loss of concentration. Currently practiced sports psychology employs conscious behavioral strategies, attempting to calm the athlete's nerves, bolster feelings of self-confidence, and help focus the competitor on the task at hand. Unfortunately, these techniques rarely have a *lasting* impact because they ignore the root causes of the problem, which are the unconsciously accumulated physical and emotional traumas.

Just like in the garden, when we pull the weeds out but leave the roots, the problem returns stronger than ever.

Injuries can at times be *directly* linked to the RSPP that the athlete struggles with. We presented the example of the ski racer unable to aggressively attack the course in competition. Instead of staying low and forward on his skis, he couldn't stop himself from leaning back and sitting high. During the prior season, he had suffered a season-ending crash in which he had torn the ACL in his right knee. This specific injury was unconsciously causing his tentativeness.

Usually, the connection of injury to performance difficulty is less clear. Athletes suffer numerous physical and emotional traumas over the years without *appearing* to have any observable negative effects on their performances. All it takes is one additional upsetting event to trigger a full scale emergence of a repetitive performance problem. For example, a high school pitching star suddenly lost his signature control and began yanking the ball into the dirt when Major League scouts attended his games. His history was replete with numerous injuries to his pitching arm, painful muscle pulls in his back, and a broken ankle suffered while sliding into a base. Upon closer examination, these accumulated injuries turned out to be the cause of his pitching yips.

Supporting our groundbreaking discovery is the fact that the brain and body automatically memorize each injury suffered by the athlete. If these traumas are not processed through, they become stuck, in their entirety, in the athlete's neurophysiology. That is, the athlete holds all of the sights, sounds, smells, emotions, and body sensations of the trauma without conscious awareness. Subsequent upsetting events then get layered upon the earlier traumas. For a period of months or even years, the athlete may appear to be totally unaffected by this accumulated trauma. This is because, up until this point, the athlete has been able to somehow adapt to the internal physical and emotional consequences of the traumas.

As additional upsetting events accumulate, however, the athlete's ability to adapt gets gradually overwhelmed. The dam holding the building pressure of the floodwaters finally weakens and springs leaks. It's at this point that the repetitive performance problem emerges visibly to the athlete, coaches, fans, and parents. Then when the athlete is under pressure to perform or is somehow unconsciously reminded of the original traumas, the dam finally breaks and the athlete is flooded with anxiety and is unable to perform even simple tasks.

Colin Burns, our Division I soccer keeper (Chapter 2), always became more fearful and tentative between the posts on a game day that was overcast and rainy. These were the exact weather conditions as when he had been kicked in the face and thus knocked out for the season, almost ending his soccer career. The reminiscent lighting, temperature, and misty rain triggered this past trauma, causing him to relive the past *without even knowing it.*

We coined the term sports traumatic stress disorder (STSD) to represent these phenomena. With STSD, whenever individuals are significantly reminded of the original trauma(s), they unknowingly are drawn back into the past. When a batter steps into the box, the fear, self-doubt, and inability to pick up the ball can be directly related to his being beaned a year earlier. The simple act of stepping up to the plate triggers an unconscious flashback. In an instant, his self-protective, fight/flight response kicks in, reflexively causing him to lean back from the plate, rush his swing, or freeze with the bat on his shoulders.

This dynamic is at the heart of every repetitive performance problem. The performance needs of the situation—in this case, stepping *toward* the ball—are short-circuited by the self-protective instinct to pull *backward.* The athlete's body maintains a frozen memory of the trauma, responding in the present as if the danger *currently* exists. These movements can be barely perceptible or can be painfully obvious, like freezing, stepping away, or lunging.

It's this conflict between the movement demands of the performance and these instinctive self-protective movements away from perceived danger that explains a pitcher who suddenly can't find the plate, a catcher who can't make the routine flip back to the pitcher, a halfback who repeatedly fumbles, a skier who slows down when needing to speed up, a golfer who jerks his wrists and blows a three-foot putt, and a gymnast who freezes whenever attempting a back handspring. Although in each of these situations, the athlete's muscle memory has been finely honed through years of skill training and repetition, the correct movement gets trumped by misfiring of the self-protective reflexes.

We recognize that our approach will be new and controversial in some quarters. Until now, repetitive sports performance problems have been conceptualized as being within the *conscious control* of the athlete. If such a thing were true, traditional sports psychology would be more effective in attaining consistent and permanent results. The fact remains that these conscious techniques by themselves are woefully inadequate in resolving trauma based RSPPs.

How can traditional sports psychology explain why Major League catcher (former Met) Mackey Sasser or Gold Glove second baseman (Yankee) Chuck Knoblauch had their careers cut short by the throwing yips? Sasser consulted with 50 professionals in a desperate attempt to overcome his throwing problems and save his career (Chapter 1). None were able to help Sasser, because not one of these professionals took a sports or personal trauma history to assess possible underlying causes.

The state-of-the-art concepts of Brainspotting Sports Work are taken from the trauma field, where those suffering from PTSD have been helped to achieve permanent relief from their symptoms. The core of our approach with RSPPs is the vulnerability of athletes to physical and emotional trauma. Every sport entails complex movements. The athlete challenges gravity, twisting and moving rapidly, and in the process collides with immovable objects and other athletes.

Many injuries occur during childhood and adolescence, a time of crucial physiological, neurological, and emotional development. Young people are far more vulnerable to trauma during these developmental periods. As a result, what happens during these times is much more likely to get locked into the young athlete's neurophysiology and emerge later as a repetitive performance problem. We have found that by using Brainspotting Sports Work, we have not only helped blocked and slumping athletes break free but also been able to lift their performances to new heights.

Our approach can also be used with athletes who are performing on par *and above* to expand their performance beyond their expectations. Even athletes at the top of their game, like Tiger Woods, are adapting around sports injuries and traumas. And *all athletes* carry the physiological, neurological, and emotional remnants of these traumas and, as a consequence, are in a constant state of adaptation. We assess all athletes on a continuum of their personal performance effectiveness. Some are on the far end as their ability to adapt has broken down and they are completely paralyzed by the yips or intractable slumps. Others are more capable of adapting to their traumas and are therefore able to perform at par, which is still below their abilities. At the far other end of the spectrum are those at the top of their games, but even these athletes can still expand their performance by identifying and processing their injuries and traumas. We have helped these competitors elevate their games beyond where they believed possible.

After 19 years of embarrassing throwing yips, Mackey Sasser (Chapter 1) is now able to comfortably throw batting practice to the junior college team that he coaches, *even when he is being watched.* As Mackey explained after his work with Dr. Grand, "I kind of feel free of the things in the past. I don't think about all the throwing problems or anything. I just throw the ball. It is more relaxed and more 'what the hell,' and to tell the truth, it's nothing major, just throwing a baseball. This is so different than when I played in the bigs."

Goal keeper Colin Burns (Chapter 2) graduated in 2005 from UMass, where he had struggled with chronic performance anxiety and loss of self-confidence. Three years after his graduation he called to let us know that he had just signed a two-year contact with the Swedish pro team Ljungskile, where, at the time of this writing, he was the *starting* keeper. Burns described his current state after the work with Dr. Goldberg: "What we did completely flipped a switch inside of me. *I'm cool and collected these days, playing in front of twenty-thousand screaming Swedes on national TV with no problem!*"

Gymnast Amanda Dearman (Chapter 6) recovered from her near career-ending injury, being frozen by fear in the gym and unable to throw the simplest of moves. She regained all her lost skills and successfully performed them anxiety-free under the pressure and scrutiny of big meets. At Regionals, she hit all four of her events to come in second in the all-around competition. In addition, Amanda continued to learn new and more challenging skills without being hampered by incapacitating fears.

Calder Kaufman, our college baseball pitcher, emerged from his work with Dr. Grand a calmer, more introspective individual. Although repeated surgeries could not resolve his multiple shoulder injuries, Calder's experience with the throwing yips was ultimately life-changing. "It was actually the best thing that could've happened to me because it forced me to directly face and conquer my anxiety, sports injury, and personal traumas. If baseball wasn't so important to me I might never have dealt with all of this." Calder's extensive work with Brainspotting Sports Work significantly changed him as a person. He is happier and far more relaxed and balanced than he ever could have imagined. He completed his undergraduate degree and is now is pursuing a master's degree in psychology. Calder aspires to work with athletes to help them overcome the same kinds of performance struggles that he faced.

We see this as a very exciting time in the field of sports psychology and performance enhancement. Brainspotting Sports Work approach is effective and powerful with athletes in all sports at every level from professional and Olympic caliber all the way to "weekend warriors." Our techniques transcend athletics and can be applied in a wide variety of endeavors including business, the performing arts, public speaking, and academics. Brainspotting Sports Work helps performers on and off the field feel better in their bodies and maintain a sense of relaxation, balance, and enhanced timing. As sports are all about breaking through barriers and rising to new heights, we believe that our methodology provides the breakthrough tools leading the way to new levels of performance expansion.

BIBLIOGRAPHY

Sports Slump Busting – 10 Steps To Mental Toughness and Peak Performance; Alan Goldberg, Ed.D.; c. 1998 Human Kinetics, Champaign, Illinois.

Emotional Healing at Warp Speed – The Power of EMDR; David Grand Ph.D.; c.2001 Harmony Books – Random House, New York, NY.

Waking The Tiger – Healing Trauma; Peter Levine, Ph. D.; c. 1997 North Atlantic Books, Berkeley, Ca.

Little Girls In Pretty Boxes – The Making and Breaking of Elite Gymnasts and Figure Skaters; Joan Ryan, c. 1995, Bantam-Doubleday Dell, New York, NY.

The Body Bears The Burden – Trauma, Dissociation and Disease; Robert Scaer MD.; c. 2001, The Haworth Medical Press, Binghamton, NY.

The Trauma Spectrum – Hidden Wounds and Human Resiliency; Robert Scaer MD. c. 2005, W.W. Norton & Company, New York, NY.

Chalked Up – Inside Elite Gymnastics' Merciless Coaching, Overzealous Parents, Eating Disorders and Elusive Olympic Dreams, Jennifer Sey, c. 2008, Harper Collins, New York, NY.

EMDR – Eye Movement Desensitization and Reprocessing: Basic Principles, 2nd Edition; Francine Shapiro; c. 2001, Guilford Press, New York, NY.

BIOGRAPHIES

Dr. G—Dr. Alan Goldberg is an international expert in the field of applied sports psychology. The former sports psychology consultant for the University of Connecticut, Dr. Goldberg has over 26 years of experience with athletes and teams across all sports at every level, from professional to junior competitors. The author of Sports Slump Busting and Playing Out Of Your Mind, Dr. G specializes in helping individuals overcome fears & blocks, snap out of slumps, and perform to their potential.
To contact Dr. Goldberg: www.competitivedge.com

Dr. Grand—Dr. Grand is a performance expert, psychotherapist, writer, lecturer, and humanitarian renown for the discovery and development of the internationally acclaimed Brainspotting. He is the author of Emotional Healing at Warp Speed. Dr. Grand is recognized for his discoveries and advancements in healing trauma and enhancing sports performance and creativity. His Brainspotting method and BioLateral Sound are now used by thousands of therapists on every continent seeking to break through the limitations of talk therapy.
To contact Dr. Grand: www.brainspotting.pro

CPSIA information can be obtained
at www.ICGtesting.com
Printed in the USA
FFOW02n0212010817
38242FF